Million Dollar Publisher

Peter Woodhead

ISBN: 978-1-8380820-0-0

First published 2020

Disclaimer

Although the author has made every effort to ensure that the information in this book is correct at press time, the author does not assume and hereby disclaims any liability to any party for any loss, damage, or disruption caused by errors or omissions, whether such errors or omissions result from negligence, accident, or any other cause. The content of this book conveys the knowledge, experiences and views of the author and does not constitute independent financial advice, mentoring or coaching.

Contents

Foreword

"It was 2003 and Yanik Silver had set up a mixed bunch of internet entrepreneurs ranging in experience from a very experienced internet marketing rock star, to a naive newbie from a totally non-marketing background (Peter Woodhead from the U.K.)"

Jim Edwards

It was early in 2003 when my good friend Yanik Silver invited me to join him on what he called a "crazy" journey with 12 internet marketers with varying degrees of experience.

Out of the 12 hopefuls in this experimental process one was from the U.K., one was from Ireland, one was from New Zealand and the rest were from the U.S.A.

Yanik had this "ideas" book full of projects he had always intended to do but never gotten around to completing.

Hence the idea of working with 12 selected partners to get the projects done and brought to market.

Yanik knew it was going to be a tall order which is where I came in. He needed an extra pair of hands to help him wrangle the crowd.

The whole project kicked off about February 2003 with the intention of all 12 projects being completed before the end of the year.

Well, long story short, all the projects did get finished and Peter Woodhead was the proverbial tortoise in the race with all the hares.

Peter was a marketing virgin. He knew diddly squat about marketing in general and internet marketing in particular. He came from an engineering background.

But he took on board all of our advice and every single day, without fail, worked on at least one aspect of his project.

He had so much to learn (like: everything) but where Peter had a BIG advantage over all the others "apprentices" was that he had no bad habits to get rid of.

We instilled into Peter the importance of writing good copy, getting to know your prospect, and converting the prospect into a customer, and, and, and ...

Peter's greatest trait was his persistence ... a bit like a dog with a bone.

When it came to launch his project, it did as well as, if not better than, most of the other, more experienced apprentices.

After the 12 months expired, most of the group kept in touch with one another, and Peter, despite living 3,000 miles away made the special effort to attend several workshops and seminars in the U.S.

Even for experienced marketers, the internet was still in its infancy back then. But Peter soaked up everything like a sponge.

Peter eventually began hosting his own workshops and seminars in the U.K.

Peter and I even held an event in London which was a huge success. Peter also co-hosted the U.K. Underground Seminar with Yanik and a copywriting workshop with the late, great, Ted Nicholas along with many of his own workshops.

Since working with Peter those first few years, we have kept in touch on a regular basis and I have kept a close eye on his progress.

Since that first project back in 2003, he went on to produce a string of websites in all manner of niches. One in particular, which he launched in 2008, did exceptionally well – Million Dollar Publisher.

Peter knew only too well how frustrating life can be as a newbie. If he hadn't had the grounding he got back in 2003, he might have easily given up.

But my guess is Peter wanted to "pay it forward" and so Million Dollar Publisher was born.

The product was a 52-week membership site which mirrored his journey from 2003 to 2008.

Million Dollar Publisher was 52 bite-sized chunks of information, delivered weekly by email, taking the newbie marketer from basic computer skills to a finished product online – baby step by baby step.

The whole idea being that each weekly part followed the previous one.

Peter took the best of that course and turned it into this book … which will help YOU make that same journey he made.

If you're looking for a step-by-step approach to changing your life by publishing your own information online, you owe it to yourself to pick up a copy of this book right now.

Jim Edwards

TheJimEdwardsMethod.com

Introduction

A Very Warm Welcome

Thank you so much for putting your faith in me by purchasing this book.

I'll try not to disappoint you.

My first aim is for you, after reading this book, to be under no illusions about publishing information online (or offline).

My second aim is for you to understand how do-able it is. Whatever you may have read, or been told, elsewhere.

Every word of what I have written has been acquired from my own experiences.

I know that it's possible to succeed. Because I've done it.

I come from an engineering background. Not knowing a damn thing about marketing. Not knowing a damn thing about persuasive copy. Not knowing a damn thing about websites.

But what I do know is that there is nothing that can't be discovered.

But don't be fooled into thinking that it's all easy, 'cos is ain't.

I always say to wannabee Information Publishers (of which I was one not too long ago), that marketing on the Internet isn't easy, which it isn't. But, it is simple.

If you follow the Steps in this book, you too will discover that some of the Steps are not easy, but they are do-able. The secret is to break them down into bite-sized chunks.

I'm a Johnny Cash fan and I like to think that if you take this Information Publishing business one piece at a time, you too will become successful. It might cost you a bit more than a dime – but not too much more.

This one book, all by itself, can't possibly make you an online publishing pro. But it can set you well on your way and on the right track.

My wish is that this book gives you the grounding that you need to get you climbing that ladder of success.

Enjoy the ride!

What This Book Is and What It's Not

Rome wasn't built in a day.

Nor can you possibly hope to grasp Information Publishing in one gulp.

You need to consume new material in bite sized chunks, and, in a particular order.

The Chapters of this introductory book (I call them Steps) are set out in a logical sequence. The order in which you should both consume them and put them into practice.

But before diving in, I recommend that you …

First, take a look at what I call the "30,000ft. view." If you're a "Newbie" to Marketing on the Internet, this short report will give you an overview of what Information Publishing is all about. (If you're not a neophyte, then you can skip this).

Next, I would recommend that you read my Special Report titled: "The Truth." No doubt you have read about, or even bought, other online marketing material. Most of which will have told you just how easy it all is.

Well, it isn't easy. But it is simple.

In my Special Report "The Truth", I blow the lid on many of the myths bandied around about making "easy" money on the Internet.

Common sense should tell you that it ain't so. Otherwise everybody would be rich. Which is clearly not the case.

However ...

...having read the above two Special Reports, you should now have a pretty good idea that working online IS worthwhile, provided you do it right.

It is a steep learning curve (or series of learning curves) but I can promise you this: it's well, well worth the effort.

You should now be ready to begin at Step #1. Make sure that you fully understand this first Step. This first Step has nothing directly to do with online publishing but everything to do with your success. It is an essential pre-requisite.

I would then recommend, that you spend some time devouring Steps #2 thru #7.

That would bring you to the stage where you need to consider your offer and your sales piece (Steps #8 and #9). Writing copy is the steepest of learning curves. It's where most people fall down.

The subject of writing good copy is way too much content to cram into this book. It's a whole subject all on its own.

There is however, a structure to good copy and you will get that here. At the end of Step #9 I have listed some books and courses on the topic of copywriting. Get some of them and don't just read them -study them.

What you need to glean from this book is that Copywriting is essential to your success in online publishing. Most people want to gloss over this Step. Big Mistake! Seriously, without good copy you will never succeed.

And that doesn't just refer to your sales copy. It refers to virtually everything that you write: sales copy, eMails, articles, blog posts, you name it.

In fact, read Step #9 TEN times. Why? Because in this Step lies the true secret to success in any marketing environment – especially online marketing.

Once you have completed Steps #8 and #9, you would now have a product and a persuasive message to sell your product. You now need to let the world know what you've got.

At this point, you will need a web presence so that your target market can see what you have to offer.

Now, pause a while!

You have created an irresistible offer and placed it in front of thousands of hungry customers. People will love it and your sales will go through the roof. Right?

Well, that's the theory. That's what everyone hopes for. But hope just doesn't cut it.

You need to take a "scientific" approach. It really is a numbers game (providing you have got the previous steps mastered).

The more you know about your "numbers" and more importantly, what you do to improve them, the more successful you will be.

Get to know the people who have bought from you and let them get to know you. If they like you, trust you, and love what you have to offer, they will come back for more.

So …

Give it to ‘em!

Ready to roll?

Then pick up that “30,000 Foot View” Special Report, get stuck in and I wish you all that I wish for myself.

Very warmly,

Peter Woodhead

Peter Woodhead

Author and Self Publisher

Ebor Publishing Limited

Step #1

You Must Have The Right Mindset If You Want to Succeed

"The elevator to success is out of order.
You'll have to use the stairs - one step at a time"

Joe Girard

Introduction

Without the right Mindset, you will be doomed to failure.

You may even think you have the right Mindset, but have you?

If you are not well-read on your chosen subject, it is unlikely that you have.

One of the best routes to getting the right Mindset is to read the works of Orison Swett Marden. Most of today's top marketers have studied him or one of his students – such as Napoleon Hill. You must have heard of him.

This subject of "Mindset" is a very complex one and studies are still being carried out on this much mis-understood topic.

It might be worthwhile defining what is meant when we talk about Mindset.

The dictionary definition of Mindset is:

"A set of beliefs or way of thinking that determine somebody's behavior and outlook"

In this Step you will discover:

- The findings of two eminent psychologists on the subject of mind-setting
- A 6 step process that will help you on your way to success
- The importance of Goal Setting

Space only allows me to scratch the surface of these topics. If you want to go deeper, I have recommended books for your further study.

Who was Abraham Maslow?

Abraham Maslow was a psychologist that came into prominence during the first half of the twentieth century.

The norm at the time for psychologists was to study people with problems. But Maslow was different.

He studied only successful people.

His assertion was that most people wanted more than what they already had. Once they had met their basic needs they would develop higher needs.

He is well-known for his "Hierarchy of Needs" consisting of five levels.

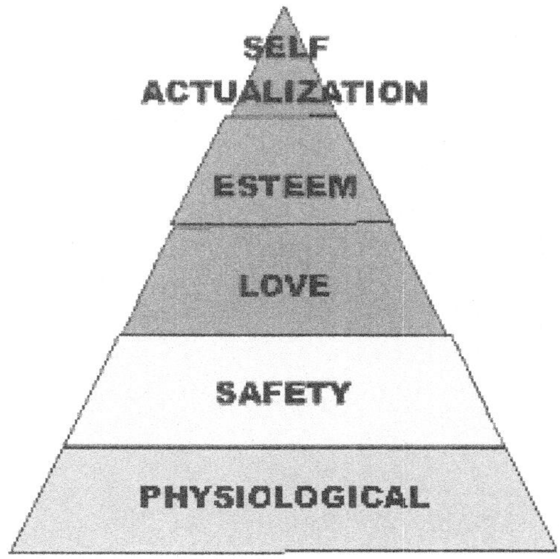

Physiological Needs

In the bottom level of the pyramid he identified basic needs. Staple requirements like food, water, and shelter.

For the entrepreneur, this could mean products on cooking or survival.

Safety and Security Needs

His next level of needs identified safety and security. His findings were that people felt unsafe at times. They want:

- freedom
- financial freedom
- to be safe from violence
- law and order
- stability.

The entrepreneur would want to target careers, fitness, health and other security type niches.

Love and Belonging Needs

Maslow found that people need to escape loneliness, to give and receive love, and have a sense of belonging. They want friendship, giving and receiving love, to care for someone, and to be cared about.

Entrepreneurs would want to create products about relationship for this niche. For example: online dating.

Self Esteem Needs

This level is where people have a need to feel valuable. To have the respect of people and to respect their peers. He found that if a person did not fulfil their self-esteem needs, they felt:

- inferior
- weak
- helpless
- worthless.

Entrepreneurs wanting to create products around this level would most likely go for the motivational niche.

Self-Development Needs

Maslow's findings were that a small group of people reached a level he called "Self- Actualization". This would be where all of their needs would be met.

Maslow's explanation of people who reached this level was that they had found their "calling."

Our entrepreneur would call this level: self-development and create educational courses, self-improvement books, etc.

Refer to Steps #5 and #7 of this book for an actual example.

Most people confuse this self-development level with fame and fortune, which is not always the case. Many psychologists believe that most people who do reach the highest level of happiness are unknown beyond their own circle of friends.

What level would your product fall into?

Once you decide on your niche, and then create a product for that niche, decide which level of the Maslow pyramid it belongs to and blend that into your marketing.

All the levels are important. You could create a product for any of them. The real secret is to connect your product to the Maslow level and make sure that you refer to it in all of your marketing.

The Findings of Carol Dweck

Dr. Carol Dweck is a more modern psychologist.

Dr.Dweck explains in her book: “Mindset” that people carry basically two types of mindset: a fixed (or static) mindset and a growth mindset.

A fixed mindset suggests that it cannot change.

Whereas a growth mindset sees disappointment as an opportunity.

Both mindsets are shown from an early age and are carried on into adulthood.

Her research has showed that kids with the growth mindset were prepared to extend themselves whereas the kids with a fixed mindset were quite happy with the status quo showing no enthusiasm.

Kids with a growth mindset were eager to extend their current knowledge and aptitude.

Even at adult age, the people with a fixed mindset were content and opposed to change. People with growth mindsets were more content, healthier, more satisfied and more prosperous.

One of the biggest findings is that people with fixed mindsets are inherently lazy. They like to go for the safe option every time.

People with growth mindsets tackle obstacles put in their way and extend themselves.

In short – the fixed mindset does not like any kind of improvement or change.

The growth mindset realises that change is inevitable and supports it.

Later in this book you will read a lot about winners and failures. In fact the percentage is a ratio of 3% to 97%.

Can you guess which type of mindset has the 3% and which type has the 97%?

Perhaps it would be worth knowing which type of mindset you had before embarking on an online information publishing business. To me it rather suggests that your success or failure is already "written in the cards".

However, there is light at the end of the tunnel. Mindsets can be changed. Everyone has elements of both kind of mindset.

Dr. Dweck's book opened my eyes and helped me understand why some things are the way they are.

Interesting stuff!

A 6 Step Process For Achieving Your Success

If you combine the right Mindset with the right knowledge, you will have the dream lifestyle.

Here are 6 pointers to help you arrive there:

1. The power of giving

   "You can have everything in life that you want, if you will just help enough other people to get what they want"

   Zig Ziglar

   - Are you passionate about helping other people?
   - People will pay good money if you can provide them with solutions
   - What you have to offer needs to be about what they want and not what you want to give them
   - By doing your research you can find out what they want

2. Your time is precious

   "Your time is more valuable than money. You can always get more money but you cannot get more time"

   Jim Rohn

   - There is only you, so find out how to leverage your time
   - You must keep track of your time

- The use of deadlines is a great way to make the most of your time
- You should charge more if people want access to your time

3. You can't do everything yourself

    - You don't have to do everything yourself, so don't even try
    - You must work on the things that you are good at and hire others to do the things that you can't do
    - If you don't get others to do the hard stuff, it could be costing you dearly in time
    - It's easy to find workers on the internet

4. You need to focus

    - You can only work on one thing at a time. Us homo sapiens are not wired for multi-tasking
    - If you have a mentor, make him or her your only one
    - Focus on developing your business
    - Focus only on what you are doing right now

5. You need to know why you are doing what you are doing

    - Why are you reading this book?
    - Why are you working towards a goal?
    - Why do you want your ideal lifestyle?
    - Why have you set a main goal?

The bigger your "why" the quicker everything will happen for you

6. You must take massive action
    - Have you got a plan?
    - What are you working on today, right now?
    - What have you got planned for today to accelerate your business?

The Importance of Goal Setting

Do not ignore the process of setting goals.

Goal setting works. So do deadlines.

Members of the 97% club never set goals. And if they did they would have set them so high that they were bound to fail.

Goals need to be set that are probable, not possible. Meaning that you need to be confident that you can achieve them.

"I want to be a millionaire this time next year" is a ludicrous goal. It's possible, but not very probable.

Here's my take on goal setting: People do not like change. It's too scary for them.

People are inexperienced and unsure of themselves. They are petrified at putting a foot wrong. It's the way we were brought up.

Listening to tapes or CDs or reading for just 30 minutes a day would help in this department. It will slowly remove any negative thoughts that you may have had.

Goal setting could be the topic of a whole new book, but I'll just give you my simplistic view here. Set yourself 3 kind of goals:

1. A 5 year goal. Don't get too ambitious. Aim for the lifestyle that you want. Perhaps multiple streams of income from your publishing business.

   Set this goal at a level that you know you can achieve.

   Several times your current income is a good a good starter. The point being is that you need to make any goal achievable. Stretch yourself – yes. Over-stretch yourself – no.

2. A short-term goal. Again, make it realistic. Something on the lines of: "I will increase my income by 100% in twelve months"

3. Add simple psychological goals:

   i) simple tasks that you know you can achieve but have never got around to doing them – this lets your brain get used to the fact that goals are actually achievable

   ii) set psychological goals that give you confidence and determination: "I can do it" goals

   iii) visualize your goals – it has been said that visualization is imagination with emotion. Visualize that you have already achieved your goals. If one of your goals is to have a new car by the end of the year, then visualize that the car is sat on your driveway.

   But you need to get really specific with your goals. Just to visualize a car on your driveway is not specific enough.

Describe that car in detail – what model? what color? what "extras" does it have? what's the top speed? Etc.

And the way that you word your goals is mega important. Word goals as if they have already happened. For example, my Jaguar e-Pace has 17" alloy wheels, heated door mirrors, rear camera, LED headlights, B&O sound system, ebony grained leather seats with flame red stitching .....

Get yourself a "vision" book and write down your goals. Take pictures where practical of your goal. Really imagine that your goals have already been achieved.

Setting goals is a paramount step in your motivational path. It has been proven to work many times.

The secret is to set realistic goals. Don't get a chronic case of millionaire-itis. There is no rule that says you cannot better your goal. But to set your goal too high is an unnecessary burden on yourself.

We have all, since childhood, been taught the opposite. We have so much negativity to get out of our systems before we can start to think positively.

Set goals and set deadlines for all of your goals. But make them achievable. You will gain a great sense of achievement allowing you to set your next goals, and then the next one.

That's the way to make real progress. One step at a time.

Conclusion

This first Step is an important one. Do not make the mistake of glossing over this.

You must have the right mindset to be able to succeed. Do not try to rush through the process of creating a product, getting online, and marketing unless you have got your mindset in the right frame.

The first time that you create your information product is a very time-consuming process. There's such a lot to get done. But when you get to work on your second, third and subsequent projects, trust me when I say: "it gets easier and easier".

At one stage I was able to churn out an offer in under a month. I do not advocate you doing that.

But what I really, really do recommend is that you master every Step until you are a master at each and every one. And by "master" I mean attention to detail.

And finally, why is it that 97% of people that try information publishing fail? Statistics have shown that 80% of people do absolutely nothing. 17% make a half-hearted attempt. And 3% are doers.

Go out of your way to get to grips with every Step of this book and you WILL be one of the 3% of the online publishing royalty.

Start right now with this first Step. You'll be glad that you did.

Your Assignments for Step #1

You will soon come to realize that every Step of this book has an Assignment as its conclusion. The reason for this is very simple, it's called: inter-action.

You can just read this book cover to cover, and that's O.K. too.

But the fact is, nothing happens until you make it happen. You have to take action. And that, for the most part, means massive action.

To be honest, this book alone will not make you into an online publishing wizard. No one book could do that.

The subject of online information publishing is a continuous process.

However, this book is designed to give you the foundations from which you can start to build an online publishing business – if that's what you want.

The idea of the Assignments at the end of each Step is to encourage you to go deeper into what could be, a very lucrative career for you.

Your Assignment for this first Step is as detailed or as simple as you want it to be. There is no limit.

Throughout this book, and indeed throughout your online publishing career (if that's what you choose to do) there should be no relaxation on your capacity to take things further.

With that in mind, if you want to be serious about this, you will need to read books, study courses, attend seminars and workshops (if not in person then via webinars etc). You must keep adding to your knowledge.

So here are your Assignments (plural) for this first Step:

1. Get yourself set up from day 1. Set yourself one long term, several medium term, many short term goals, and daily "to do" lists.
2. Get yourself down to your nearest stationery suppliers, or Amazon, and buy yourself an A5 sized notebook. Make this your "Vision Book"
3. Get yourself a daily planner. I personally use a Filofax but any planner would do the job.
4. Set yourself up with a home office. If you haven't got the space, it would have to be your kitchen table, but that's not ideal.
5. You will need some basic tools. Maybe not to begin with but as you get further down the line, some tools are just not to be without. Here is what I would recommend as an absolute minimum:
    - A good, reliable internet connection
    - A trusty computer, preferably a laptop. You will need your mobility
    - A bookcase or at least an organized place to store things

6. Here is what I would recommend you have, the sooner the better:

    - An office (at home) and a desk
    - A filing cabinet
    - A printer (non color will be OK)
    - Wall planners
    - All the necessary stationery

7. Start to build your library. If you don't like reading books etc. then you are probably not suited to the business of online information publishing. Your success in any business, will have a lot to do with your education.

    You can get motivational tapes/CDs from a company called: Nightingale Conant. If you spend a lot of time in your car, these are ideal for you.

    I am an avid reader, I get through, on average, one book per week. And in between I consume a lot of articles, magazines and the like.

    Some of the books I have read more than once. My record is somewhere around 5 times for one particular book.

    I don't know any marketers that don't read but I suppose there will be some exceptions.

    But for the rest of us, consuming works by others that have succeeded, is the way to go. I learned this lesson from one of the masters.

It is said that if you read for just one hour per day you will become an expert in your field. Just imagine what more than one hour per day could do for you!

8. Get, and read:
    - "Start With Why" by Simon Sinek
    - "Maslow's Hierarchy of Needs" by 50 Minutes
    - "Mindset" by Dr. Carol S. Dweck
    - "The 7 Habits of Highly Effective People" by Stephen R. Covey
    - "The 7 Habits of Highly Effective People: Personal Workbook" by Stephen R. Covey

So there you go. It seems a lot for your first Assignment.

The best action you can take is to consume works by master marketers. They were the true studs of the marketplace. I'm talking about Masters of yesteryear, guys like:

- John E. Kennedy
- John Caples
- Claude Hopkins
- Clyde Bedell
- Eugene Schwartz
- Robert Collier
- Rosser Reeves
- David Ogilvy

And many, many others

I'm willing to wager that the majority of the 97% that fail do not read anything at all.

I believe that is one of the main reasons of their failure.

It's O.K. getting ready to get ready, but it is real action that gets you the results.

Step #2

Why Information Publishing?

"There have been more fortunes made in publishing than in any other industry, including the stock market and real estate"

Anon

Introduction

The title of this Step is: "Why Information Publishing?"

I could just reply to that with: "Why Not?"

But that would not be very helpful at all.

I could equally say: "Why Not A 'Normal' Business Like Most 'Ordinary' People?"

Ah! Now there's a clue. That last question contained the 'B' word.

"Business"

Let's get one thing straight before you go any further into this book. And make no mistake about what I state next.

Online Information Publishing is a business. It's not a hobby.

People are in business to make money. Most bricks and mortar businesses barely make a profit. Sure, they make sales but they also have high, sometimes very high, overheads.

Some folk buy into franchises. An average franchise could set you back, say, $100,000 and you would have to toe the line of the franchisor.

I'll stand corrected, but a Macdonald's franchise could cost you upwards of $300,000

Ouch! That's a lot of burger flipping and all the staff headaches, customer queries, complaints .... The list goes on.

True, I am biased against conventional businesses, but I've seen far too many nightmares of people working 80+ hours a week and barely showing a profit at the end of it all.

My heart bleeds for them.

It's a fact that 80% of all business start-ups fail in their first 18 months. [Source: Bloomberg]

O.K. – 20% of those bricks and mortar businesses survive and prosper.

But the vast majority, all they have done is buy themselves a job.

Such a lot of businesses work on puny margins. Averaging around 10% - 15% You've got to sell $100 worth of product to make a measly $10. That might be alright for some, but no way would it be alright for online information publishing.

And I would hope that you would agree.

So what if you are hell bent on working for yourself but don't want to be a slave to your business?

The logical answer to my way of thinking is to be an entrepreneur.

Entrepreneurs Have a Great Imagination

Entrepreneurs are allowed to dream a little.

They imagine:

- Creating products once and getting paid over and over again
- Generating money at will
- Creating products for people who have a passion
- Doing only the things that they enjoy doing and outsourcing the rest to freelancers
- Taking exotic vacations and still getting paid while they are sipping pina coladas on the beach
- Having no employee hassles or vendor problems
- A 60 second commute to their office
- Low start-up costs and huge profit margins (near 100% sometimes)
- Selling products that people can buy 24/7 and 365 days of the year
- Hanging out with people that have similar imaginations

You see, they love what they do. It is the dream lifestyle for them.

I wonder why more people don't get involved.

Maybe it's because they have not heard of the benefits.

Maybe it's because they have heard some horror stories.

Maybe it's because they have also tried before and failed.

I can relate to all the reasons. I've seen it all many times over.

The fact is, there are a lot of "internet low life" out there, most of whom have not been mega-successful themselves but peddle their crap theories about this and about that.

I honestly don't know how these scroats sleep at night.

If you have read my Special Report: "The Truth About Internet Marketing" you will hear me talk about the dark side of online information publishing.

However, I am going to tell you about the bright side of this business model because it really is astonishing what can be achieved when you direct your energy and knowledge into your own online information publishing business.

Of course, there are "some" people that fail. Statistics have revealed that this is the majority. In fact, the number of people that fail at online information publishing is worse than the number of people that fail in bricks and mortar businesses.

Here are the numbers:

Bricks and mortar business:	failure rate 80%
Online information publishing business:	failure rate 97%

Wow! I bet you didn't expect that!

I know that your first question is going to be: "If the failure rate is so high, then why are you trying to convince people to get into this game?"

Great question.

And here's the answer …

The attrition rate is so high in online information publishing for a number of reasons, but the main one is that far too many people have been hood-winked into believing that it is easy.

You have only to look at the contents of this book to realize that it is anything but easy. I talk about breaking the subject down into "bite-sized chunks" but even then, some of the chunks can be a steep learning curve.

Here's a very real thing. People want instant gratification.

Wakey wakey! Life just isn't like that.

When I was at college, one of my professors put it very well (he was talking about qualifications) he said: "if it were easy, it wouldn't be worth having"

That statement is probably even more true when it comes to the topic of online information publishing. Meaning, that if it were easy, everyone would be doing it and everyone would be rich.

It isn't easy. But it is simple.

How many seminars and workshops have you been to on the topic? None, a few, or plenty?

Well I can tell you, I have been to a gazillion and hosted quite a few myself. And I can tell you that the 97% failure rate is about right. In fact, it may be higher.

So I started doing my own mini surveys. Just going around talking to people at the seminar break times etc. And those 97% of people all fell into the same category – they wanted this instant solution.

It doesn't exist. Here's what I found by performing my rather crude surveys:

In the online information publishing business, a large proportion of attendees were looking for some sort of "Get Rich Quick" program.

If any one of the speakers were offering the next "shiny object" or some "magic bullet" they would readily rush to the back of the room and gobble them up.

Some speakers at these events should behave themselves. What's the point in offering products that students will almost certainly never use?

I would agree, that if the event was on a specialist topic, then the audience might be a tad more savvy. Maybe the attendees at those events already have a website up-and-running so a neat traffic generation product might be what they are looking for.

But for people just starting out in the business a more basic approach should be provided.

Now, having said all that, is it really worth getting into the game of online information publishing? The answer is categorically – yes! But with an obvious caveat.

To make this really simple, here's an analogy. If you were having a house built you would want to plan it first. Maybe you would hire an architect unless you are one yourself. And you would build that house according to his design.

You wouldn't dream of going very far without a firm foundation. Would you?

And every step of the way, the walls, the interiors, the plumbing, the electrics, the entertainment system, the roof etc. would be all the building blocks you would need to get the project complete.

You could do a lot of the work yourself or you could simply project manage the whole thing. But what you couldn't do, is try to miss out any of the stages and get a finished house without doing any serious work.

And of course, it takes time, effort and resources.

An online publishing business is a very similar process. You cannot complete a project without putting in the time, effort and resources.

Yet most newbies think they can do just that.

There is simply no way around doing the necessary work and then spending time and resources on the marketing of your product.

It's a little bit like depositing money in the bank. You make regular deposits over time and when the time is right you are ready to make a withdrawal.

It's a shame that those 97% of people do not take a step backwards and understand what's going on. 97% is a shocking number. They don't want to spend time learning a system and they don't want to put in any effort. But they're happy to part with their hard-earned on some crazy whim.

It beggars belief.

It doesn't have to be that way.

Let's leave behind the doom and gloom and start to look at the more positive aspects. Beginning with ...

The Benefits of Being An Online Information Publisher

Work your way up to being a full-time online publisher (it could take you about 6 months working just a few hours a day) and you will be able to enjoy the following:

- No more J.O.B. – who likes living each month when there's always too much month left after the money?
- No boss – you are now the boss, no more young whip-per-snappers telling you what to do
- No employees – use outsourcers if you want to get stuff done
- No commuting – unless you class the one minute commute to your home office
- No premises – you work from home. The kitchen table if you have to at first
- Low start-up costs – forget $100,000+ franchise fees or buying large stock. How does less than $500 sound to get started?
- Virtually no risk – the only thing you are risking is your time
- You don't have to get into debt – no need for expensive bank loans
- Unlimited profit potential – profit margins as high as 99.99% are achievable but on average 80% is about the norm
- Work from anywhere in the world – I go cruising a lot. I go to Australia a lot. As long as I have an internet connection, I carry on with my business

- No discrimination against age, sex, religion, ethnic origin
- No inventory required – most of your products (if not all) will be delivered digitally
- Switch off/Switch on as required – want to take a break? Go ahead. If you have to keep tabs on your online business you can hire a virtual assistant
- Work when you want – midnight and the early hours of the morning are not uncommon for me - leaving me the rest of my day to do as I please
- Residual income – it is common for most online marketers to set up products with a recurring income. Membership sites are the ultimate online product.
- Earn money on auto-pilot – once set up, a website is like a little money pumping oil well

What Kind of Money Can You Make With Simple Websites?

Imagine that you have a $37 digital product.

After you have paid the initial costs to set your site up on the internet (around $100) your production costs are virtually nothing.

You now need to market your digital product otherwise how are people going to know that it's there? The quickest, easiest and cheapest way to do this is by advertising.

Let's put a round figure of $9 to acquire each customer. Your profit per product would look something like:

Sale of product per unit	$37

Cost per sale	$ 9
Profit	$28

If you were to sell 3 products your total profit would be $84

Say you do 9 sales a week and it starts to get interesting for you.

That could be over $1,000 a month …

From just one lowly-priced downloadable product, and it's all happened automagically, even when you were asleep in bed.

Now, what if your price was $47 or even $67?

I'll let you do the math.

If you have set up your product creation, market presence, and ordering system correctly, you can't help but make money if you drive the right kind of traffic to your website.

Now I was pretty bad at algebra at school but even I can get the following formula:

Traffic + Conversion = Sales

Roughly translated it means that if you drive the right kind of traffic to your website and your sales copy converts those visitors – you will make sales.

Imagine if you have 4 digital products priced at $37, $47, $67 and $97 respectively and you were to sell a mere 5 of each per week.

Now you do the math!

And what if you turned one of those products into a physical product, say a plain and simple CD or DVD priced at $97

Would you say that you now have the beginnings of a fantastic online business?

Your success would only be limited by the amount of targeted traffic you could send to each offer.

The above simplistic example is more than possible but you have to get every Step of the process spot on. And you will if you follow all of the Steps explained to you in this book.

I'll not beat about the bush. It will take time to do your first product because you have a whole series of baby steps to master. But I can promise you this, if you master all of the steps, you will become successful beyond your wildest dreams.

Of the 97% of people that fail, most of them are bone idle. They are not prepared to put in the graft to get all the Steps done. That is, assuming that they knew what the Steps were.

Sure, they may start with good intentions but somewhere along the path they fall by the wayside. Don't you be one of them.

So what's it to be then? Will you be a three percenter or a ninety-seven percenter?

Conclusion

I make no apologies for being blunt with you.

It's simple really.

Accept that fortunes can, and will be, made if you follow the right path to online information publishing success. Do that, and you will be a three percenter. There is no doubt about it.

Try to take short cuts and you will fail. As sure as eggs are eggs.

There is no "magic bullet" and the latest "shiny object" pedalled by charlatans will do you no good whatsoever.

I write this book after 17 years of online marketing presence.

Since around the year 1999 I always knew there was the "Holy Grail" of online riches but I didn't know how to go about things. I imagine a lot of people reading this will be in a very similar position.

I read book after book, attended a lot of seminars and workshops, but I was always one of the 97% that didn't do anything or was always "getting ready to get ready."

In short, I felt overwhelmed with everything that needed doing and always came up against an insurmountable hurdle. I needed some help but all the so-called gurus wanted to do was try to sell me their wares.

Then I had one of those "aha" moments. I was reading a book and just a few words of wisdom hit me right in my face. Those words were an analogy.

They said roughly: "If you want to learn a trade then apprentice yourself to a craftsman." Well, I already knew that because I was an engineer myself. Yes, a profession far removed from any kind of marketing, let alone online marketing.

What those words were trying to say were that if you want to learn something new, and learn it properly, then "apprentice" yourself to someone who has been there and succeeded.

I remember saying to myself at the time: "How the hell am I going to find myself a master craftsman in online marketing?"

Back in the early 2000s there were not that many masters of online marketing. Let alone any that would be prepared to mentor you – for a fee of course.

But I attended yet another seminar/workshop in London and a certain whiz kid from Maryland in the U.S. happened to be one of the speakers.

His name – Yanik Silver.

I couldn't believe how approachable he was. And to cut a long story (very) short he agreed to mentor me.

Boy, was he a task master. It took one whole year of him drumming in to me the principles of marketing, especially of the online variety. With an emphasis on copywriting.

I could so easily have given up at any point in that year. But I'm no quitter.

At the time I had a full-time job and working with Yanik took a LOT of my spare time. But I was determined not to be one of those 97%.

At the end of the year we successfully launched our product and it was a terrific success.

But the success for me in the project was not the material aspect, it was the massive education that I received in that year long experience.

I'm not for one minute suggesting that you hire someone to mentor you. I think it would be extremely difficult to do so and maybe cost prohibitive.

But this book is your starting point and a damn cheaper option.

The fact is, I have been where you are right now. I know how hard it is. I always liken the whole process to a "king-size" jigsaw puzzle.

The only way I know to getting around all the hurdles is to take each piece of the jigsaw and master it. Then, move on and master the next piece, and so on.

The bottom line to all of this is that you have to work hard and the outcome, that is, to become successful, IS worth the effort. The rewards are extraordinary.

I always say: "Get extraordinary results by doing ordinary things."

Your Assignments for Step #2

This is an easy assignment for you, but still an important one. The real work starts at Step #5.

1. Begin brainstorming potential niches for yourself, make a list. But don't go any further than just brainstorming.

   It's during these early steps that you should be preparing a background for your future online publishing business.

   Now is a good time to read around the basics.

   Get into the habit of reading books. And maybe not just business books. It's a habit that will pay BIG dividends for you.

2. Get yourself a copy of Jay Abraham's classic book: "Getting Everything You Can Out Of All You've Got" and of course, read it.

Step #3

Avoid The Biggest Causes of Failure and You Will Succeed Beyond Your Wildest Dreams

"Nothing in this world can take the place of persistence
Talent will not, nothing is more common than
unsuccessful people with talent
Genius will not, unrewarded genius is almost a proverb
Education will not, the world is full of educated derelicts
Persistence and determination alone are omnipotent
The slogan "press on" has solved, and always will solve,
the problems of the human race"

Calvin Coolidge

Introduction

What is the difference between those that succeed and those that fail?

I have observed people over the last ten years at least and noticed that people fall into categories.

Maybe I too fit into someone's category of observation.

But the fact is – 97% of people that try this online information business fall by the wayside. The big question is - why?

Over the years I have seen ordinary people with around average IQs succeed very well.

And I have seen people with well above average IQs fail miserably.

So my conclusion to those two observations are that it is not necessarily intelligence that governs how successful you will be.

I have also seen "one trick ponies" – a name given to folk who have managed to publish one product with a modicum of success but never to be seen again.

And what saddens me most of all are those "tryers" that put an enormous amount of effort into a project only to fall at one of the many hurdles that present themselves.

Many moons ago I read a little ditty about not quitting, and a line in that verse read:

"Success is failure turned inside out"

I don't have a definition for success, but if I had it would certainly contain the word "persistence" in there somewhere. I firmly believe that if you want to crack this online publishing business, or any business, then you must study it from the ground up. That is, get to know, in detail, what to do and how to do it.

And never, ever quit.

What I can say with some degree of confidence is that you will be more successful if you get rid of any bad failure habits that you have.

In this Step I have outlined 14 failure habits. There are more, but I see these 14 as the most common causes of failure.

Now, without further ado, I will outline the major failure habits that tend to get in the way.

Top Common Causes of Failure

If, perchance, you recognize yourself in any of these, get a close friend to give their honest opinion too. Either way, you have just gotta eradicate any of these habits from your system.

First up, is a common trap that almost everybody falls into:

Common Failure #1: Your Choice of Market

The late copywriting great, Gary Halbert, was once asked where he would position a hamburger stand. His answer was so obvious, but yet nobody else had thought of it.

His answer was: “Next to a starving crowd.”

What he meant was that you cannot place your hamburger stand just anywhere, you have to go where the punters go.

His analogy was extended into the marketing world and easily interpreted as meaning don’t create a product and then try to sell it. Find a market that is hungry for your product and then create a product.

You must find a market that actually wants what you have in mind. They must also have the ability to pay for it (there’s no point trying to sell anything to a starving artist).

The solution is then to find a market and then create a product to fit that market.

Step #5 is dedicated to finding the right market.

Common Failure #2: Trying to Impress

One of the major causes of failure in the bricks and mortar world of business are overheads. Keep overheads to a minimum.

I have even seen online marketers hire expensive offices just to create a good impression. Crazy. They didn't last beyond 18 months.

Common Failure #3: Partnerships

Decide right from the beginning, your online information Publishing business is just that – yours.

I have seen far too many partnerships go bad.

Go it alone. Why split all the profits? It's extremely doubtful that you would turn over more business. If it feels tempting for you to partner with someone, don't think twice about it. Think ten times.

I have seen good friendships turn sour. Ask yourself – is it worth it?

Common Failure #4: Your Business

Never forget – if you want to be serious about information publishing, and you should be, then treat it as a business. It is not a hobby.

Don't wait on this. Get in touch with an attorney or find a good accountant (or CPA) and set up your own corporation. You need that "corporate shield" to protect your personal liability.

You will then only be limited to those assets that are within your business.

Corporations, or limited companies, are cheap and easy to set up. Set yours up from the moment you get started – like right now.

Common Failure #5: Set Up The Right Business Model

Make it easy for your customers to know what business you are in. Make it clear to them how you are different, and better, than your competition.

Fedex has the slogan: "When it absolutely, positively has to be there overnight"

Nike has: "Just Do It"

Avis has: "We're No2. We try harder …"

Yours is: ???

One of the Special Reports available to you as a purchaser of this book is one about how to define your Unique Selling Proposition. And you can have a catchy slogan as well if you want.

Common Failure #6: Don't try to be a Pioneer

Pioneers are the ones that got arrows in their back.

DO NOT be a pioneer.

Do not try to create a product that no one has done before you. Marketing is far enough advanced now that everything has been tried and tested.

Do not, be afraid of competition. Competition is good. Just not too much of it.

I repeat, do not try to go into a market that is not proven. Sure, you may get lucky. But what's the chance of that? Slim or none?

Common Failure #7: Throwing in The Towel

All projects come with their obstacles.

That's why each project has to be broken down into much smaller bite sized chunks. Complete the first chunk and then move on to the next, and so on.

For me, quitting is not an option.

If Edison had quit with his light bulb experiments, you might be reading this in the dark.

Stickability is the way to go. Tackle those bite-sized chunks one at a time and you will find life much easier.

But whatever you do – don't quit.

Common Failure #8: Being a Perfectionist

You should not turn out shoddy goods, but sometimes "good enough" is good enough.

I have come across people who edit their work, and edit it again. Change this, change that. It's never good enough.

Of course you should edit your work.

Get a freelancer to proof read what you have done.

If you belong to this category you need to first recognize the fact. Always get a second pair of eyes to look over your work and then accept it's complete.

If this really is you, try to be conscious of this perfectionism and at some point, accept that what you have produced is good enough. Perfectionism can be a big time-waster. Make a big effort to stop being so fussy.

The good thing is that you will probably be a great success.

Common Failure #9: Get Rich Quick (GRQ)

Are you one of those short cut merchants that thinks there is a simple answer to making money?

If your answer is yes, I've got some really bad news for you.

GRQ does not exist. How can it? Surely, everybody would be rich if that were the case.

I'm not sorry to tell you that to be successful takes time. And effort. And resources (a.k.a money).

Get into your thick head (if it is) that there are no "silver bullets" and no "shiny objects" that promise you riches. You just cannot get something for nothing.

There is no substitute for putting in the effort.

If you feel like falling for, or already have fallen for, any kind of Get Rich Quick scheme, recognize it for what it is. Let's be logical about this. If something sounds too good to be true – it probably is.

Be honest with yourself. If you are anything like me, you will have worked hard for your money, don't give it away to some snake oil-selling scumbag.

Common Failure #10: Cynicism

If you are remotely like this persona you will never be a success. At anything.

A cynic believes that everybody does something out of suspicion.

Cynics believe nothing and no one. They are convinced that everyone is out to con them. But lucky for them, they will never get stung by a Get Rich Quick scheme.

Oscar Wilde summed up cynics with his eloquent quote:

"A cynic is someone who knows the price of everything and the value of nothing"

However, the sad thing about a cynic is that when a good offer does come along, he rejects that as well. Maybe he's just too proud or just frightened.

Common Failure #11: The Blame Culture

When things go wrong, as they often will, take ownership. Don't look around to blame others. If it is your fault, then take ownership and just move on.

Nothing's perfect. Crap happens. It may not be anyone's fault. Just sod's law.

Get on with it. Pick yourself up.

Remember: don't ever quit.

Common Failure#12: Cheating

P.T. Barnum was once credited with saying:

"There's a customer born every minute"

My favorite expression for the low-life that prey on wannabee online business owners is that they are "snake oil-selling salesmen." A derogatory term used to describe travelling salesmen selling their phoney wares to simple innocent people.

Present-day phonies use clever sales copy to give their readers a promise of the internet lifestyle. All they are doing is selling a dream.

Cheating is very similar to the Get Rich Quick category.

Again, innocent wannabees fall for it hook, line and sinker.

Don't you be one of them.

Common Failure #13: No Common Sense

It would be difficult to recognize this trait in yourself.

A family member or very good friend would put you straight on this one.

Remember the 97%?

I hate to say it but some of those 97% simply do not have the gray matter to succeed. Wanting something and actually being able to do something are not good bed mates.

A nearest and dearest should let you down gently on this one.

Some folk either have it or they don't have it. And if you don't have it, stick to the day job.

Common Failure #14: Envy

Envy is a very bad attitude. If it describes you, then you need to get it out of your system.

Why worry about the next person? Concentrate on your own business. That should give you more than enough to keep you busy. If it doesn't, then that's something else that you are doing wrong.

Instead of being envious, the success of others should inspire you to your own success.

Being envious is an emotion you need to flush out. Concentrate on your own business and maybe people will be envious of you.

Conclusion

It's strange. There are tons of books on being successful, but non about avoiding failure.

You could say that if you eliminate failure you can't help but be a success.

Hmm! Maybe.

For sure, you will be part of at least one of the categories listed previous.

Read them all and ensure that you "tick all of the boxes." Do that, and you will succeed, providing you are prepared to put in the time, effort and resources.

Having said that, being a success is not easy but if you get rid of all the common failure habits, that puts you ahead of most people. Thus allowing you to get on with your business.

Your Assignments for Step #3

1. Grab a copy of Steven Covey's resource:

   "The 7 Habits of Highly Successful People" and there is also a Personal Workbook with the same title.

   Get both resources and work your way through each of them.

Any book that sells well over 15 million copies gets my vote.

Step #4

The Psychology of Selling – People Want To Buy But They Don't Want To Be Sold To

"Approach each customer with the idea of helping him or her solve a problem or achieve a goal, not of selling a product or a service"

Brian Tracy

Introduction

This Step could possibly have been positioned just before Step #9 (Compose Your Conversion Piece) but I have deliberately placed it here early on because I think it is a powerful principle and applies to more than just your sales copy.

The techniques in this Step apply to everything that you compose:

- your sales copy
- eMails
- broadcasts
- auto-responders
- advertising – everything to do with your business.

You need to understand why people buy. And if you can understand that, then it will be easier for you to sell to them – which is your ultimate aim. Right?

It's all about human nature and that hasn't changed since the days of the cave man, but we'll not go that far back.

The art of being persuasive can be learned. You might say that some people have the gift of the gab, they are naturals at selling. Maybe, but it's more likely that they have learned their trade from somewhere.

Persuasion, as Aristotle (384-322 B.C.), defined it is:

"The art of getting people to do something they wouldn't ordinarily do if you didn't ask them"

He must have been one heck of a smart cookie, coming up with such profound wisdom all those years ago. In fact, he made it even easier for us by breaking his theory down into three distinct phases:

1. Ethos (ethical)
2. Pathos (emotional appeal)
3. Logos (logical)

Top copywriters of today still use these principles. Here's what he meant:

- Ethos – credibility exists in the minds of your readers. For your messages to be believable you must first insert some trustworthiness into the minds of your audience.
- Pathos – Or empathy. Your ability to gauge the true feelings of the people you want to deal with. Which means that you need to listen with your heart as well as your head.
- Logos – The actual words that you use. Your choice of words. The stories that you use. The quotations that you cite.

Aristotle reckoned that you should have all three of these in your message with "Logos" being the dominant one.

Fast Forward 2000 Years

What has changed in the past 2000 years?

Nothing.

People respond in exactly the same way as they did in Aristotle's day (and long before that).

We all practice persuasion at some point in our lives. And words are our basic tools. And like a good craftsman we have to select the right ones from our toolkit in order to get the job done.

Words evoke a certain feeling and a picture in the mind. And that's what you need to be able to do – get into the mind of your reader.

You will discover in Step #9 that when you write to a prospect you are writing to just one person. That person is known as your Ideal Prospect.

When writing to this ONE person doesn't mean that you are only going to send one message out. You will write to this one person because he, or she, will be your typical average prospect.

Think of being sat opposite to your typical average prospect at a table. You will be trying to put your ideas across and he, or she, will be trying to question you and raise objections. Naturally, in a conversation, you would answer these.

And so it is when writing. The difference being that when writing, you will have the opportunity to think about what you are going to write about and try to anticipate what your average prospect is going to say.

You will have ample opportunity to weave into your writings all the persuasive words that you have in your arsenal. And you should. One way to do this is to include in all of your writings some, or all, of what are known as "Psychological Triggers."

I have included another Special Report, which you can download on this topic but for space limitations I will only briefly mention them here, so that you know to look out for them. Good writers use these psychological triggers throughout their manuscripts. You should do the same.

Psychological Triggers

I include here 7 psychological triggers with a brief description of each. They are all self-explanatory and if you want to go deeper, study the Special Report of the same name.

I actually recommend that you go even deeper still and read the books on the subject that I highly recommend. The book authored by Joe Sugarman is regarded as a classic and covers 30 mind control secrets. Highly recommended.

Now, here is a synopsis of the seven psychological triggers:

1. **Tell Stories**. People love stories. Aristotle told stories too because he realized the psychological power of them. If you weave a story into your writings, people will read them providing they are of interest and on point.

2. **Reason Why.** You must always give your readers a reason why they should do something. Give them a reason why and they will respond.

3. **Specificity.** Being specific gets into the mind of your reader. 98,4% is infinitely better than saying nearly 100%
4. **The Truth.** This is also good for credibility. Your readers are not stupid. They can usually tell if you are trying to pull the wool over their eyes.
5. **Answering Objections.** Remember, when writing, you need to be writing to just that one person – your typical average prospect. Just as if they were sat right in front of you. And if they were, they would surely bombard you with questions. So, in your writings, anticipate those questions and blend them into your writings
6. **Curiosity.** I like curiosity. So much so that I recommend that you put it in any headline that you create. Add some curiosity to your compositions and people will read on because they want to know what it is that you have. It intrigues them
7. **Scarcity.** Fear of loss is great among humans. People are fearful of missing out (FOMO). Include things like "limited numbers" and "deadlines" to your copy. Prospects don't like the idea of missing out – "if he's got it then I want it too."

Conclusion

Understand what it is that makes people buy. If you can get that, then it will be so much easier to sell to them.

It is the words that you use that will get you the sales. Not fancy pictures, graphics or the like. Simply the words.

Aristotle knew this, all the marketing masters both past and present have known it, now it's your turn.

Bad copy is the number one reason that people fail. The reason being is that they have never taken the trouble to study what makes people buy.

You now have the secret to good writing. Admittedly it is a big learning curve, but in truth, even the masters are still learning. Study copywriting, and study it well, and you will profit many, many times over.

Most people don't seem to want to bother. It's too much for them. Or maybe they are just plain lazybones. Whatever the reason, don't you be one of them!

You now have the BIG secret to success online or offline. Use it.

Your Assignments For Step #4

1. Study the Special Report available to you on this topic.
2. Understand why people buy and the main psychological triggers that you should always build into your copy.
3. Get, and read, Joe Sugarman's book: "Psychological Triggers"
4. Continue to build your library

Step #5

Find a Need, Fill It and Dominate Your Market Niche

"Don't find customers for your products, find products for your customers."

Seth Godin

Introduction

Remember the Gary Halbert quote when asked where would he place his hamburger stand?

He said he would place his mobile hamburger van near a starving crowd.

Roughly translated, what he was cryptically referring to was finding a market that wants your product first, and then create a product to fit that market.

There was once a book titled: "The Lazy Man's Way To Riches" by a guy called Joe Karbo. His main thought was to sell a simple product at a low price to a gazillion people.

I'm sorry Joe, I know you sold millions of copies of that book but you got the whole principle wrong.

The correct practice is to sell a high value offer to a small group of passionate people, who can afford to pay for it (i.e. they have a credit/debit card), and who also can be marketed to easily and cheaply.

And that group of people is referred to as a niche.

I was going to slip in here the dictionary definition of a niche, but I couldn't find a better way of describing a niche than that just given.

You may already have in mind what topic you want to create an offer for. Or at least think you do. But, do you?

Everybody should go through the first stage of any new project. And that is – Research.

But before I delve into research, I would like to dissect that definition of a niche.

The Elements of a Niche

1. What is a 'high value' offer?

Perhaps the word 'high' is a little mis-leading here. What I really mean is higher priced offer. Trying to sell your offer for peanuts in the hope of selling a million is stupid if you only think about it.

You will discover later on in this book that getting traffic to your website will be the lifeblood of your business. But you will find that getting the right, targeted traffic is not easy, or cheap.

The answer, of course, is to sell fewer copies of whatever it is you want to sell to an interested group of people.

Remember also, that your offer will be the first that you create. Often referred to as your 'Front End' offer. You are, at this early stage establishing yourself.

Your offer price will not be peanuts it will be in the $37 - £97 range.

2. A small group of passionate people

Have you ever heard of the saying: “Try to sell to everyone and you’ll end up selling to no-one” ?

It’s a true statement. Only big corporations can sell cheap and to the masses. Think Walmart.

You and I are small fry by comparison. This principle of targeting a small market is tried and tested. Why re-invent the wheel? Follow the tried and tested route. Find your niche and dominate it.

If the people in your niche are enthusiastic they will already be sold. Selling a product that is of interest to them (but it’s got to be good) should be a formality.

3. Who can afford to pay for it

This may seem a little obvious but there are newbie marketers out there that still think they can market their offer to all and sundry. It takes time, effort and resources to reach a prospect, don’t waste your marketing spend on ‘starving artists’ who are nothing more than ‘freebie’ seekers.

In fact, get that freebie mentality out of your mind right now. If you think that giving away products is a way of attracting future customers then I urge you to think again. If you condition people to getting too much information for free, that is all they will ever want. Be careful.

When you get into your research you will see how to identify potential customers that do have the money, because they will have bought something previously.

4. **Can be easily contacted**

In the old days. Before t'internet, savvy marketers bought lists of people from organizations called 'list brokers' and they are still around. Lists are available for every conceivable type of prospect and/or customer.

For example, if your niche were to be 'model trains' there would be lists for model train enquirers, model train past buyers, and model train anythings.

List brokers made it easy for you to contact your target audience.

List broking is still thriving today.

The modern-day equivalent is online advertising. Pay-per-click being the most popular. Step #16 deals with this in much more detail.

Suffice it to say that your target market can be contacted quite easily.

Other things to look out for would be:

- Are there any generic magazines about your intended niche
- Does your intended niche have any forums or Facebook groups (if so, join them and just listen to what is going on)

5. Can be marketed to cheaply

Marketing isn't cheap. Directly, or indirectly, it costs money. Doesn't it make sense to target the right kind of traffic for the minimum of outlay?

Part of your research criteria will be the cost of acquiring a prospect.

Step #15 will go deeper into the detail of converting that 'prospect' into a 'customer' and what is a fair price to pay in building your list.

I hope now that you 'get it' with regard to identifying a tight niche.

Here are a few ways you can contact your target market:

- eMail
- Forums
- Facebook Groups
- Press Releases
- Classified Ads in Trade Magazines
- Direct Mail

But concentrate on just one or two to begin with.

How To Research a Niche

I can picture your thoughts right now. You've got this great idea for a product that will sell like gangbusters. Or so you think.

Maybe it will. Maybe it won't.

The first thing you have to do is research to prove that there is a market that would want your fantastic product.

It's a fact – most people think that this fantastic product idea of theirs will be wanted by everybody and has the potential to sell millions.

That would be nice but unfortunately it doesn't work quite like that.

Before you even get into research, ask: "What kind of market would be popular?"

"What market has enough people, with enough resource (money) to buy what I want to sell to them?

Before doing any research, ask yourself what are your own interests or hobbies? Surely, if you're interested in something, there must be others that share the same interest?

Ask yourself: "What is your work experience?"

Ask yourself: "What do you aspire to be? What are your goals? And ambitions?"

Take a little of your time to complete the table below. Don't skip this, you may uncover some real gems. List your work experience, hobbies and interests, and then fill out the ideas column.

Work Experience	Hobbies	Interests	Ideas

Take a simple example to demonstrate what you should be looking for. Let's use "Golf" as our example. Admittedly, golf is a niche market but it is a very broad market. What you as an information publisher are looking for, are markets that are not only smaller, but are not too big either.

Golf is a massive market. You wouldn't stand a chance if you tried to create and market a golf product. But that's not to say don't do it, you just have to drill down into the golf niche and find a smaller sub-niche. For example, golf clubs, golf carts, golf vacations, mini golf. I'm sure you've got the idea.

But sometimes, even those sub-niches are too big. Looking at the above: golf vacations could be a massive market. Maybe too big for what you want. You would maybe need to find a sub-sub-niche of golf to stand any chance of success.

Without doing any research just now, perhaps "Florida Golf Vacations" or "Learn to Play Golf Vacations" would be about right.

The more specific you get the more targeted will be your audience.

So how do you tell what is a small niche and what is a big niche? That, is the whole point of this Step.

Now we can start doing some research.

There are tools you can use to dig deep and find these "Goldilocks" niches. That's just my little term for niches that are not too small, or not too big, but just right.

Let's just re-cap what we are looking for. We are looking for a niche that:

- Has a hungry market
- Has people that are passionate

- Has people that have the money to spend (i.e. will probably have a credit/debit card)
- Is not too large
- Is not too small

Before you look for evidence that you have a viable market it is important to remember that you should not try to appease people who do not share your passion.

It is worth pointing out that the criteria you need to be looking for is a niche that has sufficient demand but also little competition. That doesn't mean no competition. Competition is good, just not too much of it.

If your niche is going to be in the area of golf, don't try to contact people that are interested in fly-fishing. You need to direct all your energies to your soul mates.

Cast your mind back to Step #4, people will only buy what they want, not what they need. It is your first job to identify a niche that really wants what you can create for them.

Then, and only then, should you create that product.

How then, do you find your "Goldilocks" niche?

I mentioned earlier that there are tools to help you find your niche – some free and some paid for. I'll keep it real simple for you and go with a free tool.

My tool of choice is a product by none other than Google.

It is called the Google Keyword Planner. It is free but you will require a Google account to access it.

Using Google's Keyword Planner

Using Google's Keyword Planner I searched for "Golf" and found that the Google tool returned a daily total of 5089 searches for the term "golf" which represents 152,670 (5089 x 30) over a month.

But on scrolling down to the bottom of the search results I found that a total of 1,439,130 searches were performed for golf related items.

That's a huge market which also means it is a very competitive market. And competition in this particular market means that there will be some BIG players. You do not want to pit yourself against such competition. They have deep pockets.

So if golf is too big a niche, what about the sub niches that we mentioned earlier?

"Golf Clubs" had 63,210 searches per month, whereas "Mini Golf" had 32,760 searches. Either of these sub-niches would be acceptable.

The bottom line is, and this is a rough approximation, as there will always be exceptions, but a niche with 100,000 searches per month could be a maximum with around 30,000 searches per month as a minimum.

There is a paid for tool that I really like – Wordtracker. Their costs range from $27 per month to $99 per month, but if you plan on doing a lot of keyword research, it is well, well worth it. They also have a 7 day free trial.

http://freekeywords.wordtracker.com

The Importance of These First Steps

Back in Step #3 you read about causes of failure in the online publishing business. Another cause of failure is the reluctance of many wannabee marketers to complete these first steps.

I have been there. Done that. And now I want to convey to you that you must not skip these first steps. They are the basics that you must have in place if you want to belong to the 3% club.

Think of the foundations of a building. You must have firm foundations.

Finding the niche that is right for you will be crucial to your success.

Here's another example for you. A little off topic but nevertheless, a lesson well learned.

Don't forget, people will buy what they want. Not what they need. Or what you think they want. What you think that they want is irrelevant. It's what your prospect thinks that counts.

It is far easier to sell to people's wants than it is to sell to their needs.

Look at it another way, it is easier to sell a solution to a problem than it is to sell a prevention to the problem.

This can be illustrated with a very simple example. Say a woman suffers from headaches, maybe it's migraine.

When she gets such an attack she will do anything to make the pain go away.

If you tried to sell some magic pill to women to prevent them getting headaches in the first place, it would prove to be a difficult sell.

The explanation is because people want immediate satisfaction. They want a solution to a problem. And they want it now! Instant gratification.

They want the cure. Prevention is a difficult sell.

Another example that we have all experienced is life insurance. People need it, but they don't really want it. That's why life insurance is one of the hardest things to sell.

Just ask your man from the Pru.

A Word About Keywords

Do not make the mistake of thinking that a high search volume translates to more sales. How would you know that these 'browsers' are buyers? They may be doing research or just curious. Volume can be a good thing but it is the conversion of the keywords that will determine your success.

Will your visitors who found you via a particular keyword opt-in to your list? Or will they buy your offer? Or are they just plain nosy and having a snoop around?

Keyword research is not to be taken lightly. That's why the word 'research' is used.

The more research you do, the better will be your results.

Look for what are termed 'long tail keywords'. These are those 4 and 5 word keyword phrases. You will not only find them easier to rank high for but they will be cheaper also.

Some marketers I know use nothing other than long tail keywords.

Typical Niche Markets and Niches To Avoid

Here is a list of some typical niche markets. You may not be turned on by any of them, but the list may spark some thought for you:

- Making money
- astrology
- Health (herbal remedies, natural cures)
- Cooking
- Magic
- Exercise and fitness
- Handicrafts
- Anti-aging
- Human psychology
- Weight loss
- Investing

There are a few niches that you should stay away from, some for legal reasons, some for unsavoury reasons, these are:

- Business Opportunities
- Medical
- Legal
- Financial

The first one in this list has a bad rep. You know, the 'Get Rich Quick' brigade.

The other three are specialist areas where you are not allowed to give advice unless you are qualified to do so. For us lay persons, leave well alone. There are hundreds, if not thousands, of other niches to have a go at.

My favorite kind of niches are "evergreen" niches. Niches that will never go out of fashion. Do not be tempted to delve into fads – the "here today, gone tomorrow" kind of niches.

You want to build an asset that will serve you for many, many years.

The Competition

It's a fairly simple job to check on competition. Just Google the niche that is of interest to you.

This will reveal the number of web pages that are on the internet. But don't forget the internet is now a mature medium and the number of web pages on any given subject will be huge (in the millions or even billions). But everything is relative.

Golf, for example, at the time of my research had over 2 Billion web pages.

Just proving that the golf niche is w-a-y too broad.

Golf clubs on the other hand, returned a search of 110,000 (close enough to meet my criteria) and had average competition with advertising costs less than 40 cents per click (all revealed on the free Google Keyword Planner tool).

Of course, you would need to do a lot more research than just the examples given here.

Looking at another niche – Hypnosis.

Using my keyword planner I discovered that the word "hypnosis" returned 135,000 searches. A tad on the high side, but I might want to go with that since any further drilling down in that niche revealed searches of around 15,000 and lower. Definitely too small.

I also found that competition in this niche was below average but it was definitely worth pursuing since advertising costs were a shade over $1 per click. Which is not too expensive, but not that cheap either.

Depending on the keyword tool that you use, assessing the competition gives varying results. That's why I like Wordtracker. It's all there in an easy-to-understand language.

And finally, one more niche - Success.

For sure, this is a highly competitive niche. Everybody wants success.

Do some research on Amazon alone and you will find umpteen resources.

But I have an idea. Because of all the works I have discovered in the Public Domain, and continue to do so, I thought I would delve a little deeper. A sort of find a niche within a niche, within a niche.

Everybody's heard of Napoleon Hill, his books have been re-published by many. But what about the guy who taught him? What was his name?

As it happens, as a result of my being "into" Public Domain works, I was familiar with this man. He was the founder of the modern success movement. So who better to build a product around than the very man who started it all.

I first thought of 'Success Secrets'. Not bad. But it proved to be still too broad. What about 'Lost Success Secrets'? Better – but variations on that theme had already been tried (just look on Amazon).

Then I hit on 'Long Lost Success Secrets'.

You see, I'd already had a fabulous success with a website called: 'Long Lost Marketing Secrets' in the next Step (#6) you will witness me trying to grab the Domain Name.

Other Places To Research

I'm a big fan of a site called "Clickbank" (see also Step #12).

Clickbank is an online source for people who want to sell their downloadable products. That would be us then.

They have a section of their website called the "Clickbank Marketplace" which gives you a very good idea of what is available and what is selling.

They do have strong competition, but Clickbank have been in existence for a long time (since 1998). They are particularly good at allowing affiliates (see Step #13) to market their members' products.

Take a good snoop around the Clickbank website. It might just jog your mind about a niche that you have given no thought to.

Another site similar to Clickbank is JVZoo:

www.JVZoo.com

A Typical Product

I will imagine that I have done my due diligence as described in this Step and found that one of my top interests is being a success in business.

A big topic, but a very interesting one.

Most people want to be a success, therefore a product that helps people reach that goal should sell very well.

In the next Step (#6) I will register a (fictitious) Domain Name.

And in Step #7 I will attempt to find a product that will be popular in that niche.

Can you remember our friend Abraham Maslow from Step #1?

His findings resulted in his "hierarchy of needs". A pyramid with five levels. The top level of his pyramid he called: "Self Actualization"

Maslow's explanation of people who reached this level was that they had satisfied everything else in their lives and wanted something "extra"

As entrepreneurs, we would call this level: "self-development" and thus create products to satisfy that need.

This is the level at which our niche will pitch to.

Conclusion

Do not dismiss this Step.

It is an extremely important one. Get involved in the wrong niche and you could be spending many hours fruitlessly.

Chance are, you already have a good idea of what you want to promote. If that's so, you are not excused doing the research. It is important that you do your due diligence.

You want to be sure, with some degree of certainty, that your chosen niche is viable. Your chances of success will be multiplied by doing so.

If you don't do the research you will be stumbling in the dark.

To summarize this Step, doing minimum research is simple. You need to, as minimum, do the following for your chosen niche:

- Check the overall demand of your proposed niche (needs ideally to be between 30,000 and 100,000 searches)
- Check the competition (it's a good thing to have competition, but not too much of it)
- Check the cost of advertising (if people are advertising it is a sure sign that the niche is workable)

If you diligently perform all the research steps described here you can be confident that your niche will be viable. It is now down to you to provide a great offer for your new niche (see Step #8)

The final word on finding a niche:

- You probably have the knowledge in your head that people will find valuable.
- Give them that knowledge in exchange for a fair value

Your Assignments for Step #5

You must know what's coming next!

To be certain here are your Assignments for this Step:

1. Complete the table shown in the text previously
2. Check the following for at least 3 of the niches that you have identified:
    - The overall demand
    - The competition
    - The cost of advertising
3. Visit Clickbank and any other similar websites to see what niches are already in the marketplace
4. However difficult it may be, choose just one niche that you will run with.
5. Get, and read, "Finding Niches Made Easy" by Christine Clayfield.

N.B. Christine Clayfield has authored several best-selling books in the online marketing field. Her book: "From Newbie To Millionaire" was another best seller.

Step #6

Register a Domain Name That Acts Like a 24 Hour Salesman For You and Tie It To Reliable Hosting

"If your business is not on the internet, then your business will be out of business"

Bill Gates

Introduction

If you've read every Step of this book so far, and completed all the assignments, you are now about to really get your feet wet.

You need to prepare yourself for getting online.

It may sound complicated if this is your first time but like all things, if the process is broken down into bite-sized chunks, it looks a lot more do-able.

You need to make your web presence visible for people searching the internet.

You do that with what's called a Domain Name.

You simply cannot go ahead choosing a Domain Name until you have firmly settled on a niche. You will of course have done this in the previous Step.

So what is a Domain Name?

A novel way of understanding a Domain Name is to use the analogy that it is like the title deed to your website.

Like all the Steps in this book, you cannot race through without giving due thought. Every Step is paramount.

Registering a Domain Name requires a lot of thought. And planning.

Think Google, Disney, Coca-Cola, McDonald's. They are not just names they are "brands".

Some people think that a name is a brand. A name is only part of a brand.

Some people think that a company logo means brand. Again, not so. A company logo may be associated with a brand, but it is not a brand.

Then what is a brand if it isn't a name or a logo?

Your Brand

Your "Brand" is what your name means to your target market. How well is your company trusted? How good are your products? How do you look after your customers?

You've identified your niche. Your next move is to dominate your niche. Your next move after that is to consistently strive to be the best at everything that you do.

Your "brand" needs to be identified in everything that you do. In your Domain Name, in your Logo. In everything that you do from now on. You have to prove yourself and remain squeeky-clean, honest, trustworthy, a provider of products that under-promise and over-deliver. You must always focus on your customer.

I shall return to the topic of branding in Step #11

The task in hand right now is to find a domain name.

Your Main Keyword

In the previous Step you did a considerable amount of research. Didn't you?

Part of that research was concerned with keywords. With one being dominant.

Examples of Golf, Hypnosis and Success were given but these would not necessarily be the main keywords. For example, "golf" was way to broad a market, so a lesser searched-for term was looked for. Something along the lines of golf carts or golf clubs.

In the case of Hypnosis – I suggested the sub-niche: Self Hypnosis.

And in the case of Success, I toyed with "Success Secrets" but that was too broad also and I settled for a three-word phrase: Lost Success Secrets.

These two and three-word expressions become what are commonly known as a "keyword phrases".

Going back 10 or even 5 years, Google liked to see this keyword phrase in your Domain Name. Search Engine experts now agree that it is no longer advantageous to have your main keyword phrase in your domain.

However, that's not to say don't do it. I'm of the opinion that the jury's still out.

Search engines still like to see what has become known as a brandable domain name.

How to Select a Brandable Domain Name

Google likes to see short domain names. The shorter the better.

However, all the short domains are taken.

Before I outline a procedure for brainstorming a great brandable domain, there are a few criteria that are recommended.

Here's a list of basic criteria recommended for domain names:

- Domains must be as short as possible (10-12 characters or less)
- Domains should be memorable and "catchy" if possible
- Domains should be a .com extension unless there is a good reason otherwise
- Domains should NOT be hyphenated
- Domains should preferably not contain numerals
- Domains should avoid abbreviations
- Domains should avoid mis-spellings
- Domains should avoid trademarks (a trademark check is easy to perform)
- Domains should avoid superlatives (words like best, no.1, etc)
- Adjectives are good in domain names – a marketing word with fizz
- Avoid the use of double/triple letters e.g. golfsuccesssecrets.com

- The domain ideally should be available as your Facebook and other social media usernames

You may have heard of domain name generators.

It is much better to brainstorm a domain name than it is to use a domain name generator. Most marketers recommend the use of domain name generators but I just find that the "manual" approach is just as good, if not better.

An example of a brandable domain for the golf cart niche might be:

GolfCartExpert.com or LuxuryGolfCarts.com or GolfClubCarrier.com

And for the Hypnosis niche: SelfHypnosis.com

And for the Success niche:

LostSuccessSecrets.com or LongLostSuccessSecrets.com

(Assuming that they are all available)

Sidenote: You may come across the term "url" (uniform resource locator). A Domain Name and url are not quite the same animal.

A domain name, as mentioned before, takes the form: yourwebsite.com

A "url" on the other hand, takes the form: yoursite.com/about_us.html. See the difference?

N.B. The ".com" extension is known as a top-level domain. Other top-level domains are ".net", ".org", etc.

Where to Register Your New Domain Name

You may by now have picked what you consider to be an awesome branded domain. You must now check to see if it is available to buy.

There are literally hundreds of domain name registrars (places where you can check availability, and purchase domain names). But my preference is to go with one of the big boys. They have been around since the internet ice age and I have had an account with them since 2001.

Their name: GoDaddy.com

Sign up for an account. If you intend to get serious about this online business, you are going to need a domain registrar account.

Sign up now. And log in.

Even without an account, GoDaddy lets you search for an available domain name. But once you have found a domain, you will need an account before you can register a name.

Domain names are cheap. And domain name registrars will do their best to reel you in with special first year offers. Click “no thanks” to all of them and go straight to their shopping cart.

Suppose you wanted to be in the “golf cart” niche. I’m not a golfer but I have a lot of friends who are and they are fanatics. Quite the epitome of a niche market.

At the time of writing this book, I quickly did a search for GolfCarts.com and, surprise, surprise, it has been taken. Probably years ago. So too was LuxuryGolfCarts.com.

However, the domain: GolfClubCarrier.com was available.

SelfHypnosis.com was taken but LongLostSuccessSecrets.com was available. This Success Secrets domain unfortunately has the “triple s” However, I would make an exception and buy it. It would make a good brand.

You could experiment with something like: LongLostSecretsofSuccess.com but then it starts to get more than a little awkward. A four-keyword phrase is cumbersome enough, but a five-keyword phrase?

Fictitious examples, but they illustrate the procedure.

Once you decide to buy a domain of your choice you will be offered a very cheap price for the first year. But don’t be taken in by this. Subsequent years will be considerably more.

For how long a period should you register a domain for? Great question.

I’ll try to give you a great answer.

It is not known for sure, but Google possibly recognizes domains with a long registration. Likewise, Google recognizes domains that have been registered for some time. Whether they add weight to your listing for these facts is not readily known – but it is suspected so.

Does it therefore not make sense to register your domain for the longest possible period? You might think, I’m not sure that this product is going to be a blockbuster, so I’ll only register the domain for one year.

Quite frankly, with the cost of domains I wouldn't worry about this. I register my main domains for 10 years at a time. I then know that I have peace of mind, whatever Google ranks for or doesn't rank for.

Now here's another point to take cognizance of. If your first or second choice of domain are taken, GoDaddy, and all the other domain registrars, will try to sell you the .net, .org, .info, .biz or indeed any other top level domain.

Unless you have a very good reason to do otherwise, e.g. you want the .co.uk or .au extension, then do not be tempted to register anything other than the .com extension.

There are two main reasons for this. Firstly, .com is recognized by everyone, especially in the US (everyone's major marketplace) as THE domain extension. All others are considered second rate.

Secondly, if you were to opt for say, the .net extension there would be confusion between your website and the person who owns the .com version. Why would you want to confuse your market?

One last word on domain name registration.

Once you have decided to buy your .com domain name, your registrar will take you on a journey before you can finally get to the checkout page. And on that journey they will try to up-sell you on all things domain-wise. Items such as domain name privacy and protection, domain name security, more domain extensions, eMail account, website builders, and lastly the biggy, they offer you web hosting.

You should NOT be tempted into signing up for ANY of these services.

Hit the "no thanks" buttons and go straight to checkout and pay for your domain(s) only.

Hosting is the next topic and it is important that your domain name registration and your hosting are kept separate from each other. That means, you do not buy them from the same source.

Setting up your hosting

You have now set up an address for your information website you now need to make that information accessible to all and sundry.

You need to set up a hosting account.

Just like domain registrars, there are hundreds, if not thousands of web hosting providers.

A web host is a company that "stores" the content of your website(s) on its own servers.

Before you purchase hosting for your website, all of your files are still sat on your computer. There is no way the world wide public can access the information you will have so diligently prepared for them.

You need to get those files transferred from your computer's hard drive up to your hosting company's servers by what is called "File Transfer Protocol." That's just a fancy name for up-loading files from one place to another.

Here are 3 questions for you, would you like your website available for everyone to see:

- All the time?
- Some of the time?
- Most of the time?

Of course, you would want your website to be available all of the time, or as near to 100% of the time. Therefore, it stands to reason that you should not take web hosting lightly.

You are running a business not a hobby.

If your website is inaccessible, you will lose the respect of your readership and even more importantly, you will lose customers.

You need good, professional web hosting. Not some back-street amateur set up.

Online information publishing, to do it right, is all about being professional. This is going to be your business, maybe a full-time business.

If you were to set up a traditional bricks-and-mortar business you would have the scourge of all businesses – overheads. Your online information publishing business will be no different. You will have overheads.

It ain't free.

But it ain't expensive either. The cost of setting up your online business will be a fraction of a fraction of any bricks-and-mortar business.

One of the bigger costs of your online business will be web hosting. You have just got to get it right first time. You can really go el cheapo on hosting and get it for free. But how efficient and professional is that going to be?

Yep, you guessed it. Free hosting is for little old ladies and their knitting hobby site. It most certainly is not for you. Be prepared to pay for the best. You will be surprised at how cost-effective web hosting can be. Even the best.

You need to order your web hosting from a trust-worthy provider who has been around a long time. Even the best web host will not be able to keep you online 100% of the time. Servers need maintenance, just like most things. But 99.99% is pretty close.

I have used many web hosts since I have been online and the big boys that have a proven track record are my choice.

Before I reveal my choice of web hosting for you there is one detail that your hosting absolutely must have. It must have what is called "cPanel" Most good hosting companies do have cPanel, but beware, some do not.

As a beginner I would use a company called Hostgator. They have their critics, but so does any web host. You can access their website at:

www.GetHostgator.com

They have basically three plans:

- Hatchling plan – you can host one website
- Baby plan – you can host unlimited websites
- Business plan – you can host unlimited websites with extra tools

I keep harping on about your presence online is a business and not a hobby. This is especially so when it comes to the hosting package that you choose.

It will be highly likely that you will publish more than one website, so that would rule out the Hatchling plan. That leaves you with a choice between the Baby Plan and the Business Plan.

But never forget – you are running a business, not a hobby.

Your choice needs to be the Business Plan. It has got that little bit extra.

For both your Domain Name and your Hosting – pay yearly. Avoid monthly payments.

When registering for your hosting, you will be asked to select a domain name. You have already purchased a domain name from GoDaddy.com - so use that.

N.B. I mentioned this earlier in this Step but it is so important that I will mention it again here. You need to order your domain name from a different provider than you order your web hosting. The reason being that if anything were to go wrong, which would be extremely unlikely, you would not have all your eggs in one basket.

You will need to sign in to your account. If you have not yet got an account, create one.

Make all payments using your company debit card.

You will almost immediately receive an eMail from your web host. You will need the contents of this eMail for the next section.

Tip: You have now taken two of the most basic but important steps in your online business and you may already have noticed that for each one, you received a username and password. Do not try to commit these to memory. More usernames and passwords will be coming your way for various matters.

I find the best way to keep track of usernames and passwords is to save them. Either digitally or hard copy. I do both.

The software I use to keep all my useful information can be found at:

www.Roboform.com

It's free. And for my hard copy I make a note in a neat little notepad readily available from Amazon (there goes another username and password).

Connecting your domain name to your web hosting

You are nearly there. Just a minor detail to attend to.

Have you put your usernames and passwords in a safe place? Do not continue until you have done so. Until I disciplined myself into saving these, I used to get myself into a right royal mess.

Got your eMail from Hostgator? Good! Print it out or write it down.

Now, log back in to your GoDaddy account. From the drop-down menu select: "My Domains"

For this next stage your domain needs to be un-locked. But don't forget to lock it when you are done.

Look for: "Name Servers" they will be set to some default name. These need to be changed.

Refer to the eMail sent to you by Hostgator. That eMail will contain the Name Servers for your hosting account. There will be two references in that eMail in the form of:

Nsxxx.hostgator.com

Nsyyy.hostgator.com

These are called Domain Name Servers or DNS.

Within GoDaddy you need to over-write the two default DNS with the ones that were sent to you by Hostgator.

GoDaddy may give you options:

- Parked Nameservers
- Hosting Nameservers
- Custom Nameservers

Choose "Custom Nameservers" and replace "Nameserver1" and "Nameserver2" with the two DNS that were sent to you by Hostgator.

Then hit "OK" and you will be re-directed to a page that states your changes have been submitted – please wait a few minutes for your changes to take effect.

You should soon see that the Nameservers you just entered are now on your GoDaddy account.

It can take up to 48 hours before your website will propagate to your new host, in practice this is usually within 24 hours.

You should now re-lock your domain in your GoDaddy account.

You are now all set to transfer information from your computer to your web host's server.

That's it. It's as easy as that. You now have a web presence. All that you need to do now is create a product (on your own computer) and transfer those files to your web hosting when you are ready to do so.

Conclusion

After you complete this Step, and take the necessary action, you are well on your way to being online.

This Step is effectively, the "set-up" stage.

In this Step you discovered how to:

- Brainstorm a brandable domain name
- Open an account with GoDaddy.com
- Register a domain name with a .com extension
- Set up a Business Plan account with: www.GetHostgator.com
- Store your usernames and passwords in a safe, secure place
- Connect your domain name to your web hosting

Now that the rubber has firmly hit the road, it is time to create a product to match the niche that you have identified.

Step #7 will identify three ways that I create a product. And I do it without too much effort on my part. And in double-quick time. And, in keeping with my low budget policy, at little or even no cost.

Step #7 is an important Step, but it is also a simple Step. And if you haven't seen my methods before, you are in for a big surprise.

N.B. GetHostgator.com is an affiliate link which means that if you order through that link I will receive a small commission. It doesn't cost you any more, and may even be cheaper.

Your Assignments for Step #6

It's pretty obvious what your assignments are for this Step. But I'll list them anyways:

1. Brainstorm at least three domain names that are brandable around your main keyword phrase
2. Open an account at GoDaddy.com
3. Register one of your chosen domains with the .com extension and consider two other extension for the same name
4. Set up a Business Plan account with: www.GetHostgator.com
5. Get yourself a safe place to store all of your usernames and passwords (you'd better do this or live to regret it later)
6. Tie your domain name to your web hosting as described in this Step

7. Sign up for Roboform and get yourself a hard copy of the "Internet Address & Password Logbook"

There, how easy was all that?

Step #7

Create Your Information Product That Will Be Unique – No One Else Will Have What You've Got

"Good products can be sold by honest advertising. If you don't think the product is good, you have no business to be advertising it."

David Ogilvy

Introduction

Creating products is the easy part of online information publishing.

If you haven't seen my presentations before then you are in for a real eye-opener.

Firstly though, I'd like to give you my criteria for creating products:

1. They must be unique, i.e. nobody else, anywhere will have the exact same product
2. They must be quick to create
3. They must cost little to create

You will notice that I use the word "create" when I talk about producing products. That means that I rarely "make" a product from a blank canvas. Although here are always exceptions.

Creating a product is easy. Making a product is hard work.

In a nutshell, I create the majority of my products from three sources. One in particular. It's all perfectly legal and ethical.

The three sources that I use are:

1. The Public Domain
2. Private Label Rights
3. Licensed Products

There is a fourth source that I use (outsourcing), but I almost never use this source for creating a product. But I do use it for getting the things done that I can't do or don't want to do.

If your product were to be anything but a book, then Outsourcing the work could be a very good option. I use Outsourcing for all of my graphics, for creating software, and some website design, shopping cart set ups, etc.

You may have also heard me talk about Front End products and Back End products.

Let me explain just a bit more. Your Front End product will be the first one that you create for that particular niche.

I will talk more about your Back End products in Steps #10 and #18, but put simply they are follow-up products that are usually higher priced than your Front End.

Front End products will typically be derived from the Public Domain and/or Private Label Rights.

Back End Products can be anything you want them to be. You can easily find something in the Public Domain, some sort of Private Label rights package, or a Licensed Product.

This current Step in the process will concentrate on you creating a typical Front End product and for that I would usually create my product with a terrific work from the Public Domain. I may use a Private Label product, I would almost certainly never use a Licensed Product (I usually only use Licensed Products for Back End offers).

Right now, you're probably thinking to yourself, what the heck are Public Domain products, Private Label Rights, and Licensed Products?

So let me put that straight right now.

Public Domain products

If you have a need to create the content for your website but you haven't got the time, the inclination, or the knowledge to write your own material (and let's face it, how many of us have got the time?) then I've got some really good news for you.

There are a ton of works that are freely available. Yes, you read that right – free!

They are free because they are no longer protected by Copyright (or they were never copyrighted in the first place). And when I mention a ton of material, I mean literally millions. In fact, it is estimated that there are over 2 Billion works languishing in the Public domain.

All these works that are not protected by copyright are said to be "in the Public Domain." You may have heard the term before but not appreciated what it meant.

For example, all the well-known "classics" are in the Public Domain. Works by Shakespeare, Dickens, Mark Twain, Ernest Hemingway, and many, many others.

Some of them may never have had any Copyright, or if they had it will have expired.

"Public Domain" simply means that a work is free to use by the general public. That means you and I.

To really understand Public Domain you need to first understand a little bit about Copyright.

Any work that is written is Copyright. From the moment you put pen to paper. The fact that you maybe do not register the Copyright does not matter.

What is good news for us online publishers is that Copyright does not last forever.

Copyright expires with time.

There are some fantastic works in the Public Domain, on all manner of subjects, and in all forms (not just books) just waiting for you to re-discover and resurrect them.

What kind of works are in the Public Domain?

- They could be old (like Shakespeare and Dickens) that were published before there was ever any Copyright law
- They could be works where the Copyright has expired

- They could be works that were gifted to the public (e.g. P.T. Barnum's auto-biography)
- They could be works written by the United States Federal Government employees
- They could be academic works

To make the understanding of Public Domain easier, I will primarily concentrate on written works but the Public Domain covers many other areas, including but not limited to:

- Videos
- Films
- Articles
- Research
- Illustrations
- Photographs
- Maps

The United States is by far the largest market, so when I refer to Copyright law I will be using the rules applicable to the United States. Other countries vary slightly but are mainly similar.

I find the best way to explain Copyright and its relation to the Public Domain is with the following table (Table 7.1). The table is up-to-date as of July 2020. The date 1924 will change to 1925 on January 1st. 2021 and from 1925 to 1926 on January 1st. 2022 and so on.

Table 7.1

Date of Work	Copyright Duration
Published before January 1st. 1924	Work is in the Public Domain
Published between 1924-1963 (and if the Copyright was not renewed)	Work is in the Public Domain
Published between 1924-1963 (and if the Copyright was renewed)	95 years from date of publication
Published after 1963	95 years from date of publication
Created, but not published before 1978	Life of the author plus 70 years
Created (or published) 1978 or later	Life of the author plus 70 years but not before 2047

The first date is very clear. Anything published before January 1st. 1924 is in the Public Domain (until recently, this date was January 1st. 1923).

Anything published between 1st. January 1924 and 31st. December 1963 is a somewhat gray area.

The reason it was a gray area was because of a weird rule about Copyright. Works published during this period (1924 -1964) had to have their Copyright renewed in the 28th. year after publication otherwise the Copyright would expire.

As you can expect, a lot of them did expire. And those are the works that are of interest to us. Those are the works that are in the Public Domain.

For those that did remember to renew their Copyrights, they remained protected for a further 47 years (but more on that little later).

Not surprisingly, it is estimated that around 85% of works published in this period were not renewed (would you remember to renew something after 28 years?). Those works are therefore in the Public Domain and are free for you to find and do what you want with.

However, there is a little bit of work involved (but not too difficult) in order to segregate the 85% of works that are estimated to not having their Copyright renewed from the 15% that did have their Copyright renewed.

This is crucial. You must do this due diligence to prove that a work is truly in the Public Domain.

And trust me on this. There are some absolute gems. Works that were best-sellers in their day.

Here's what my good friend Ted Nicholas had to say about these works:

> "Peter,
>
> You have done a great job of breathing life back to these old works. Books written all those years ago were not just good then they were even better than books written today.
>
> Don't stop doing it, I know you find some real nuggets of gold."
>
> Ted Nicholas
>
> Billion Dollar Publisher

If you refer to Table 7.1 you will find the following:

Works published on, or after, January 1st. 1964 are protected by Copyright and are therefore not in the Public Domain. But eventually, even the Copyright on these works will expire (in 95 years)

However, if a work was created, but never published before 1978, they will not enter the Public Domain until 70 years after the death of the author. Obviously, such works are of no interest to us as information publishers.

Finally, if a work was either created, or published, after 1978, that work will not fall into the Public Domain for the life of the author, plus 70 years, but at the earliest by 2047.

These works are clearly of no interest to us either.

Where can you find Public Domain Works?

There are many places to look for Public Domain material. You may read about some of them elsewhere. But, be careful. It is so easy to think you have found a P.D. work only to discover later (maybe after you've spent time and money) that it is not P.D.

I look at many places in my quest for a P.D. product but in general, I only use four resources:

4. Alibris
5. ABE Books
6. U.S. Federal Government websites
7. Wikipedia

I'll very quickly show you how I locate products from these websites:

Source #1: Alibris This is a book finding resource and can be found at:

www.Alibris.com

You will be required to sign up for this service, but it's free. Get your username and password book at the ready.

You don't need to sign up in order to complete a search but you will be required to create an account should you wish to purchase any of your findings.

There is a little trick with this site for finding what we want – in the search box enter your keyword phrase plus the words "pre 1964"

Failure to do that will return searches of modern-day reprints which is not what you want. You want an original copy.

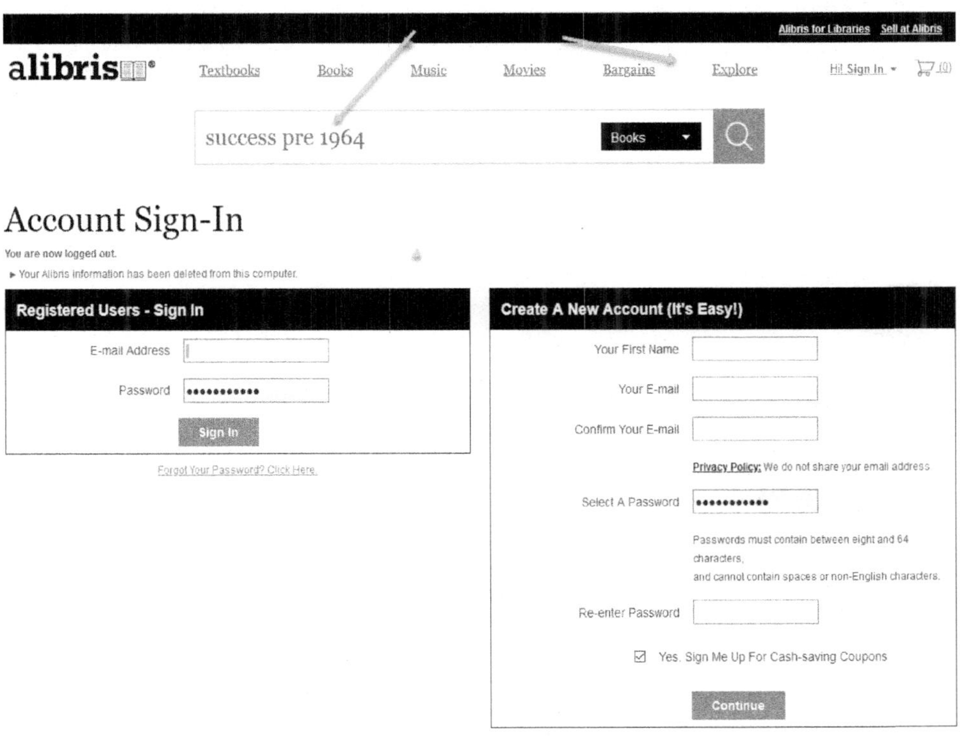

Hit "continue" and you will be taken to another screen where you can narrow down your search.

As it happens, and to make the whole process very simple, all that you need to do are fill in the "keyword" field and the year of publication field. Which in our case will be "before 1964"

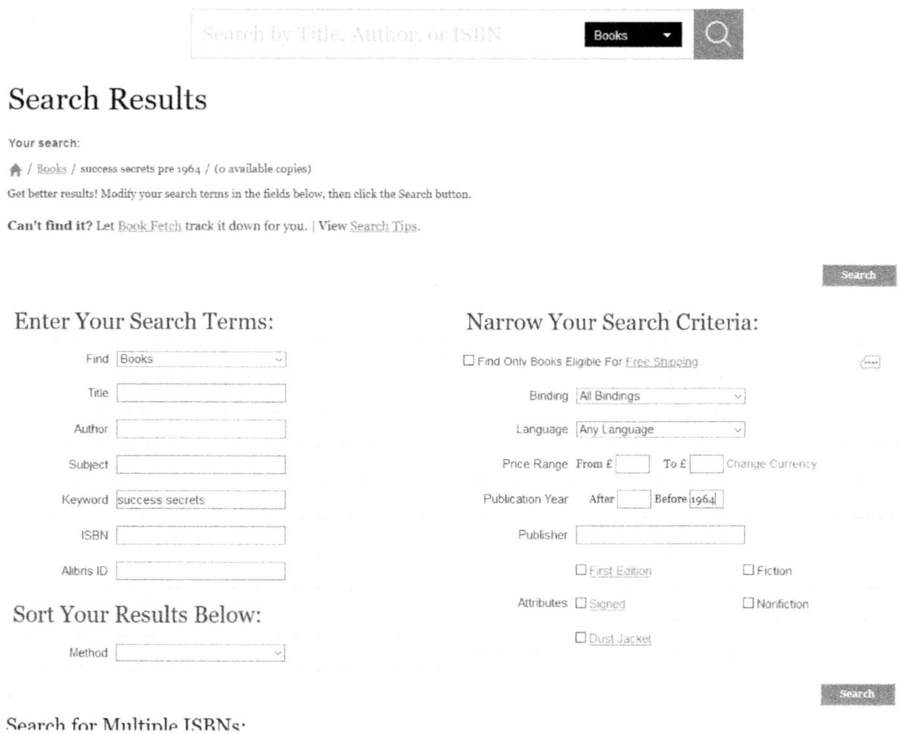

This will then reveal, depending on the niche you have chosen, several pages of pre-1964 works by various authors.

You may recognize some of them and in particular you may recognize some of the publishers.

Tip: You can do another search under author and/or publisher, this new search would reveal even more results.

However, not to deflate you, but all that you have located so far is a pre-1964 resource. It is not necessarily in the Public Domain.

You now have to do your due diligence to prove that what you intend to use is indeed a Public Domain work.

Source #2: ABE Books. This is another book finding resource and the one that I tend to use the most. Website:

www.ABEBooks.com

Very similar to Alibris but in my opinion, better.

But I'll let you decide which is the better of the two.

You need to select: Advanced Search

And fill in the field for "keyword" and in the field "published before" enter 1964

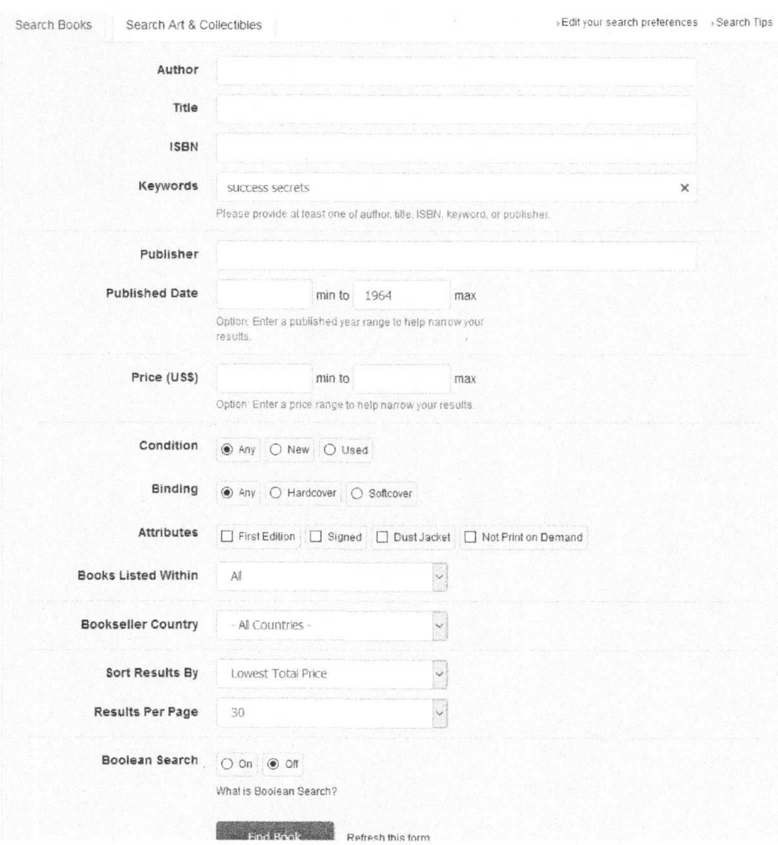

You could enter more fields but just the keyword and the published year should be sufficient.

The hit the "Find Book" icon and the ABE search engine will go to work and find you plenty of books (depending on your niche).

I just find this resource more user-friendly than Alibris and also it tends to reveal more and better resouces.

Source #3: U.S. Federal Government websites.

There are two U.S. Federal Government websites that I have utilized, and they are a great source of recent information on just about every topic under the sun.

The first of these is: https://www.FTC.gov

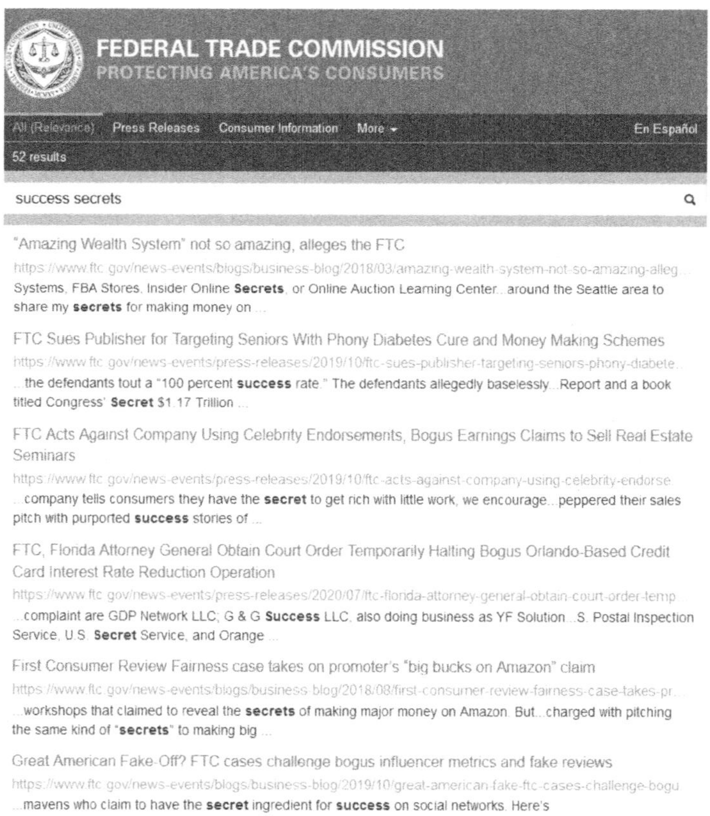

And the second is: https://www.FirstGov.gov

Very similar to the above website.

A treasure trove of useful material, most of which is free to use.

Source #4: Wikipedia.

Wikipedia is protected by what is known as a GNU license. Which means that you can take the content and re-use it, but in its original form you cannot use it and Copyright the material.

The material on Wikipedia is a free resource but it cannot be copyrighted.

However, you can take the content and re-word it. If you completely change the original wording into your own you would then be free to copyright the material.

Source #5: There are other websites which I don't use anymore but they may be a source of ideas. I will list them here for your reference:

- www.Bookfinder.com
  Very general and limited. You need to know the name of the author and the title.
- www. DoverPublications.com
  You can search this site by category. Only really useful for research. But note: do not buy books from this site as you may not receive an original copy which is what you must have.
- www.KessingerPublishing.com
  Similar to above

- www.Gutenberg.net
  Project Gutenberg has been around a long time. It is no good for fining Public Domain material despite what others may tell you.

For original Public Domain material you need to search either Alibris or ABEBooks and even then, you must ensure that works have not been renewed. It is your responsibility to do these checks.

Private Label Rights (PLR)

By definition, Private Label Rights are a license to which an author sells his rights to the intellectual property of their work. The author defines the extent of the rights he grants but it is usual for PLR products to be granted with full publishing rights.

Usually, there are many buyers of PLR products making the price very low. But a note of caution is also required, a lot of PLR is absolute crap. Only buy PLR from a source known to you, or recommended by a friend.

A PLR license can be used to create eBooks, articles, software, graphics, video, complete newsletters, and in fact the only limit is your imagination.

Each license usually permits the buyer to re-brand the content under their own livery.

If and when I re-purpose PLR material, I would normally improve the content to my satisfaction (so I would make sure that any license allows me to do that). More than likely, even when improved upon, any PLR product that I use would be as a bonus item. But don't forget, it still has to be useful and of value.

I also would make sure that my license allows me to not just modify the content but to also re-sell that modified content.

Licensed Products

Because I have paid substantial fees to obtain the rights to products (both digital and physical) I generally reserve such products for use in my Back End i.e. more expensive products.

Good and more expensive products are not cheap to create. And they can take a lot of time to bring to market.

It only makes sense to at least consider licensing your Back End products.

Without going into too much detail here, the subject of Back End products will be dealt with in more details in Step #18

Suffice it to say here that, in general, Back End products are generally of much greater value than Front End products.

Licensing products makes the creation process quick and easy, and, because time is money, very cost effective.

Outsourcing

Outsourcing very simply is a business practice whereby a company, or individual, hires another individual, or company, to develop and/or create products that would normally be accomplished "in-house."

Usually tasks are outsourced because the hiring party can't do the work or doesn't want to do the work.

There may be a secondary reason for companies to outsource, and that is – it is cheaper to do so.

The practice of outsourcing became popular in the 1980s and has grown into a massive industry today.

I admit, I outsource a lot of tasks. I don't really have much option. I am not a jack of all trades. I cannot do everything. I'll have a go at most things but ask me to do, for example, a logo or some other graphics and – forget it. I just can't do it.

Therefore, I outsource such tasks.

Can I do programming? I can hardly spell it, let alone do it. No, it's horses for courses for me. Give it to the experts.

My experiences with outsourcing are quite extensive and I have been outsourcing right from the beginning of my online career – very early 2000s.

Here are some of the outsourcers I would recommend, apologies if I have missed out some good ones but I can only go on what I have tried:

- Upwork.com
- Freelancer.com
- Guru.com
- Fiverr.com

All the above are very competent. And I have had good work from a company based in the Philippines:

www.OnlineJobs.ph

Theoretically, you could outsource <u>everything</u> but you would really need to know what you were doing.

My Hypothetical Website

Back in Step #5 I identified “Success” as a broad niche. Then I narrowed it down to “Success Secrets” and drilled down even further to the sub-sub-niche of “Lost Success Secrets”.

I wasn’t too comfortable with that as I knew that several marketers had launched products around the “Lost Success Secrets” theme so I decided to delve even deeper. To find something truly unique.

I came up with the idea of “Long Lost Success Secrets” which kinda fitted the bill as I intended using Public Domain material. Which meant finding a product, or products, that were published pre 1964.

And, I had previously experienced fabulous success with a website titled:

www.LongLostMarketingSecrets.com

I also thought that a lot of marketers have heard of Napoleon Hill and that there are many books re-published in his name. I’m sure you too have heard of his most famous work: “Think and Grow Rich”?

[As an aside, there were many editions of this work. For some strange reason, all the other editions’ copyright were renewed. But not the 1937 edition]

I wasn’t too keen on even trying to use this work. I want to be unique.

Then I thought that every craftsman must have a mentor, a kind of “master and apprentice” relationship. If Napoleon Hill was the apprentice, then who was his master?

I happen to have done a lot of research on the master, he was known as the founder of the modern "Success Movement" – his name: Orison Swett Marden from way back in the nineteenth century.

And no, he didn't have a master. He was completely self-taught.

To cut a really long story short, Orison Swett Marden had a shocking up-bringing. He survived adversity after adversity and still managed to author over 80 books.

A truly remarkable man.

However, when he was young, he somehow got hold of a masterpiece that he studied, and studied, and then studied some more.

It is that masterpiece that made him the man that he was.

Not only did he go on to author over 80 books but he also founded the prestigious 'Success Magazine'. A publication that is still in circulation today.

Next time you are in your favorite bookstore, treat yourself to a copy.

The masterpiece that Marden read and read was called: "Self Help" by Samuel Smiles. It is that work that I have decided to use as the main product for my "new" website.

Conclusion

You should now be convinced that you have to produce first rate products if you want to survive in the online information publishing business.

Just any product won't cut it in today's market. People are not as gullible as they used to be. They have sharp B.S. detectors.

Yep, there still exists 'Get Rich Quick Merchants' plying their "trade" but they don't last long.

You, as an information publisher, want to be in this business for the long haul. You have to act and be seen as honest and trust-worthy. Produce unique and high-quality materials and you will not go far wrong.

Treat your customers well and they will treat you well by not just buying your products but recommending you to others.

Always, always under-promise and over-deliver.

Read the Special Report titled: "How to Compose Your Unique Selling Proposition (USP)" and live up to it.

In this Step I found a core resource, "Self Help" by Samuel Smiles, for a fictitious product in order to demonstrate the process.

Your Assignments for Step #7

At the risk of repeating myself, please don't just read these Assignments. The way to true success is to take action.

If you must, read the book in its entirety, but do yourself a favor and come back to complete the Assignments. Only by taking action will you ever progress.

I've been where you are right now. You have to take action.

Here are your action steps for this Step:

1. Acquaint yourself with what is Public Domain. It is a real treasure trove of information. Almost for sure, that whatever niche you intend to get into, the Public Domain will have something for you.

   Spend some time familiarising yourself with searching for P.D. material. It could be the best use of your time.

   Find a good product that fits your niche.

2. Briefly read up on Private Label Rights and Licensed products. There are PLR products for almost all niches. It's

worth having a look around, there may just be something to fit the niche that you are in.

By all means check out Licensed products, but Step #18 will deal with this topic in more detail.

3. This Step is about creating an information product. Take what you have found in 1. above and turn it into a product. I assume that product will be a written work i.e. a book. The preferred way to create a book is to use Public Domain content.

   Do your due diligence to make sure the book is Public Domain.

   Obtain an original copy of the book. Then, in order to get a copy of the book:

   Option1: Get the book scanned by a professional scanning company. You will require the scanned copy in 'Word' format.

   Option 2: Type out the contents of the book (or get someone to do it for you) and then modify it enough to make the work unique to you. If the author is famous, leave his/her name on the resource. If not, replace the author's name with your own, or you can use a pseudonym.

   Turn your completed item into PDF format ready for inclusion in your offer.

4. Get, and read, the following books:

   - "The Public Domain" by Stephen Fishman

- “Resell Rights Profits” by Leigh Burke
- “Start Now, Get Perfect Later” by Rob Moore
- “The Lean Start-Up” by Eric Ries

Step #8

Make Your Offer So Irresistible That Your Prospects Have Just Gotta Have It

"I'm gonna make you an offer you can't refuse"

Jimmy Helms

Introduction

Let's just re-cap a little. If you read my Special Report – "The 30,000 Foot View" you may remember that I crudely broke down the whole process of creating, publishing and marketing an information product into three sections:

- A Beginning – the creation of your product
- A Middle – getting your product online
- An End – The marketing of your product

The first 7 Steps of this book have been about the preparation for, and the creation of, your product.

The next 5 Steps will progress your masterpiece from "drawing board" to the internet.

As it stands right now, nobody knows that you have just created a blockbuster product.

It is now time to position your product where it can be seen by everyone.

The information product you have created in Step #7 will be terrific.

However, merely offering one product to your potential customers will not be enough.

You need to be making an offer to your potential customer that is a no-brainer. An offer that they can't refuse or say "no" to. An offer they simply must have.

You need to make an "irresistible" offer.

Your "Irresistible Offer

You will make your offer irresistible by creating not just one, but a bundle of products, all related to the main product that you created in Step #7.

And to sweeten the pot even more, you will add bonuses to your main offer. Not just any bonuses, but unique bonuses that could stand alone as a product.

There is a saying in the marketing world: "If you can't sell it – then you can't give it away either."

Yes, you read that correctly. You may end up with an offer that comprises of not one or two products, but three or four and, three or four bonus products. Your "bundle" of products could be five, six, seven or more individual products.

But it is important that each one has value, and be difficult, or impossible to find anywhere else.

If you create your products from the Public Domain, your uniqueness will be assured. Why? Because with Public Domain material you can make all the changes you like to your works, and you should. The more changes that you make, the more unique will be your product. And, if you make "substantial" changes you are allowed to Copyright your new work.

The next Step (#9) will cover the composing of your sales letter. Or copy as it is called. And there is a very good reason why you will be creating your irresistible offer before you compose your copy.

That reason is so that you will be able to write your copy around your offer.

If you recall, back in Step #5 we defined a niche. And in Step #7 we created one "hard-to-find" product to fit that niche. It's now time to find some more products, related to that niche, to make our offer "irresistible."

You will also recall that our chosen niche was "Lost Success Secrets" and the domain: LongLostSuccessSecrets.com was available. [Just for insurance I thought I would register this domain name in case anybody else stumbled across it. Whether I'll do anything with it, remains to be seen]

You also discovered that the easiest, fastest, and cheapest way to create a product was to look in three places:

- The Public Domain
- Private Label Rights
- Licensed Products

For our first product we decided to find a hard-to-find classic from the Public Domain.

I did a little brainstorming and decided that a modern day success guru was a little too common and we decided to look back in time and discover who was one of the very first pioneers of the success movement.

I thought of Napoleon Hill. Everybody's heard of him. Haven't they?

But then I thought, wait a mo! Napoleon Hill must have gotten his information from some other guru. So I did some digging and the name "Orison Swett Marden" came up.

It turned out that this fellow had a shocking up-bringing and many, many setbacks in life and still went on to author over 80 books. All of them best sellers in their day.

It turned out that he was known as the Founder of the Modern Day Success Movement. And the Founder of Success Magazine that is still going to this day.

I became a bit of an expert in all things Orison Swett Marden. I read a dozen or so of his books, some were a tad on the stodgy side, but some were real gems.

So I picked one as the main product. See Step #7 (the previous Step) for the details.

The title of this work was: "Self Help"

You see, I thought I'd try the same trick that I did with Napoleon Hill and find the mentor of Orison Swett Marden, only to find that he never had a mentor. He was 100% self-taught.

He learned all that he knew from an old book.

O.K. books back then (19th Century) were not written in the same style as books are written today, but their content was good.

In fact, a lot of today's success gurus take their methods from these very books. What better testimonial is there than that?

One book, as good as 'Self Help' is, will not be good enough as an offer.

Doing further research revealed a plethora of books about success. I had to dig deep to sought the wheat from the chaf. It took time. Lots of it.

This Step is about cobbling together a bundle so as to make an offer that is irresistible to the reader.

Researching the Public Domain is one option, but it's not the only option.

I could find a Private Resale Right resource, or I could look to license a product, or I could get something completely new written by outsourcing it to the likes of Fiverr or Upwork.

The remainder of this Step is dedicated to what I think will make a darn good package.

I am thinking on the lines of adding another three resources to the Self Help book for the main offer, a couple of bonus products, and an up-sell (of which you will learn more about in Step #10).

As I alluded to a few paragraphs back, I have a few options from where I can find the products for my package:

- The Public Domain
- Private Resale Rights
- Licensed Products
- Outsourcing

Here are the results of my Public Domain search:

- "How To Make Your Daydreams Come True" by Elmer Wheeler
- "How To Put Yourself Across" by Elmer Wheeler
- "He Can Who Thinks He Can" by Orison Swett Marden
- "Training For Efficiency" by Orison Swett Marden
- "Victorious Attitude" by Orison Swett Marden
- "Pushing To The Front" by Orison Swett Marden
- "Think and Grow Rich" by Napoleon Hill (1937 edition only)
- "Secrets of The Ages" by Robert Collier
- "The Game of Life and How To Play It" by Florence Scovel Shinn
- "The Three Keys To Success" by Lord Beaverbrook
- "You're Better Than You Think" by Dora Albert
- "Success Through a Positive Mental Attitude" by Clement Stone
- "The Power of Positive Thinking" by Norman Vincent Peale
- "Self Reliance" by Ralph Waldo Emerson

N.B. The use of any of the above must be checked for copyright renewal. You must do your own due diligence if you intend to use any of the above works.

Here are a few licensed products that I already have:

- "The Midas Method" by Stuart Goldsmith
- "Seven Secrets of The Millionaires" by Stuart Goldsmith

I haven't looked into Private Label Rights too deeply as I am of the opinion that the above list is enough to go on – for now.

There might even be a couple of titles in the above list that you recognize. "Think and Grow Rich" by Napoleon Hill is the obvious one. But it would have to be the hard-to-get 1937 edition for it to be copyright free and therefore legal.

At this stage, there are a couple of other options which I didn't mention. One is the possibility of making an audio file as one of the products or as a bonus. The other is including a video of some kind – also as a bonus.

And a further thought is to take a really good book, for example "Think and Grow Rich" and make a summary of the book either as a mini booklet or using a PowerPoint presentation with the use of bullet points.

And yet another option would be to interview one of today's success gurus. It's not as hard as you think. I have done several interviews with gurus in other niches. A transcript or even a recording of the interview would be the resulting product.

The possibilities are endless. You are only limited by your own imagination. So get your thinking cap on!

Back to formulating an irresistible offer.

What I am trying to accomplish is create a product bundle with "Self Help" as the main product.

Stop press! I just did another search and found a couple of resources "hiding" on my hard drive which I could use as bonuses. I'd completely forgot I had these.

The first of these is a collection of cards by Orison Swett Marden called: "Success Nuggets". I suppose today's description of these would be flash cards.

The other resource I found was a boxed set of 24 mini booklets titled "National Success Course"

Old fashioned they may be, but I've scrutinized these resources and there is a lot of useful information within them. They are definitely on my "possibility list."

However, I haven't ordered any of the books as yet so I have no idea whether they are good, bad, or somewhere in between.

But, in this particular case, I am familiar with all of the authors and so I would not be too worried about using any of them.

So now the time has come for me to make a choice. Which works do I pick to be part of my irresistible offer?

It's a tough call because I could make a case for all of them. However, too many is almost as bad as not enough.

Here's my choice, you may have thought otherwise, in which case do your own research and produce your own product.

The Main Offer

My main offer would comprise of the following:

- **"Self Help"** by Samuel Smiles (the main product from Step #7)
- **"How to Make Your Daydreams Come True"** by Elmer Wheeler
- **"The Game of Life and How To Play It"** by Florence Scovel Shinn
- **"He Can Who Thinks He Can"** by Orison Swett Marden

Adding Value

And then I would add three bonuses:

- **"Seven Secrets of The Millionaires"** by Stuart Goldsmith
- **"The Midas Method"** by Stuart Goldsmith
- **A PowerPoint Summary of Think and Grow Rich** by Napoleon Hill

I will deal later in this book with how you can sell more from your website at the point of sale (Step #10) but for now, just accept the term "up-sell" as a mechanism for selling more product.

And for this "up-sell" I would propose to do something very different. I would offer a multi-part course on the topic in question delivered over say, 10 months.

Meaning that customers who bought your main offer and opted for the "up-sell" would receive the following:

- 4 titles (your main offer)

- Another 3 titles (your bonuses)
- A ten-part monthly course for those that opted for the "up-sell"

Does all that sound irresistible?

I will conclude this Step with a comment about pricing.

Pricing Your Offer

First, ask yourself: "What would you be willing to pay for such a bundle of unique and hard-to-find resources?"

Remember, the complete offer, including the "up-sell," would be delivered digitally, which means that you will have no postage costs and no printing costs. Just the selling fees that Clickbank (see Step #12) would charge and your advertising costs.

You could offer your bundle at $47, $67, $97 or maybe more. And the "up-sell" could be marketed for say, $20 per month.

But whatever you chose, you'd be guessing. And guessing is not very scientific.

I don't know what you should charge for this package. Nobody would. What you must do is test the market. And that's a whole new ball game covered in the final section of this book (Steps #13 - #17). The marketing section.

My "gut" feeling is to go with $67 for the main offer and $17 per month for the "up-sell." This will be confirmed when you test. And you MUST test (see Step #15).

Conclusion

Finally, when you get to Step #18 you may want to think about a Back End product in this niche. Not wanting to complicate matters right now, but I'll leave the subject of a "Back End" product until then.

I will end this Step with a lead into the next Step (#9) which is the "Composing of Your Conversion Piece" a.k.a. your Sales Copy.

This next Step is arguably the most important Step of them all.

Psst! Do you want to know a secret?

Let me explain.

To be successful at information publishing, you need to be a whiz at algebra.

Understand this "complex" algebraic formula and you'll get it. Guaranteed!

traffic + conversion = sales

I'll refer back to that formula many times. Because if you understand that one simple formula, then your success will be assured.

In this "complex" equation, the "conversion" element is your sales copy.

The above equation is absolutely spot on. No ifs. No buts.

Drive traffic to your website. Convert that traffic with your visitors clicking on the buy button, and you can't help but make sales.

To be more accurate, the equation should read:

Targeted traffic + (an irresistible offer + good sales copy)
= lots of ale

Which means: drive the right kind of traffic to your website, have a great offer, and a good piece of sales copy and you can't help but make sales.

Simple, eh?

Then why do so many people fail?

Answer: because they get one or more of the components of that simple formula wrong. There can be no other explanation.

Maybe you've guessed it already. It's 99,99% always the sales copy that is not good enough.

It's time now to move on to that all-important topic – your sales copy. See you in the next Step.

Your Assignments for Step #8:

Your assignment for this Step is a straight-forward one.

Having found your main product in the previous Step you now have to create your irresistible offer.

If you follow everything that I did in this Step you will end up with an offer similar to the one I did.

You now know what an irresistible offer should comprise of so go on, get your imagination going, and put together a package that you think the prospects in your niche would rave about.

The example in this Step is just an example, you don't have to follow it exactly.

Get creative.

1. Use the websites detailed to you in the previous Step and go and find your own golden nuggets.

They are out there. There are over 2 Billion works, (yes that's Billion with a capital 'B') in the Public Domain alone.

Go on, rummage out those best sellers of yesteryear and make for yourself a fantastic bundle of resources.

2. Get, and read: "The Irresistible Offer" by Mark Joyner

Step #9

Compose Persuasive Sales Copy That Will Convert Your Visitors Into Rabid Buyers

"Make it simple. Make it memorable. Make it inviting to look at. Make it fun to read."

Leo Burnett

Introduction

For sure, your sales copy, or just "copy" as it's called, will make or break you.

Without good copy you will sell few, if any, products.

Take another look at the simple formula from Step #8:

traffic + conversion = sales

It's the "conversion" element of that formula that your sales copy is responsible for.

If your sales copy is good, you will "convert" your visitors into sales.

If your sales copy is sub-standard you will convert few visitors into sales. If any.

Being able to write good, persuasive copy is a very special skill. But it can be learned, and it must be learned.

This is the Step where most people fail. Because it takes some effort.

Don't be one of them. Spend time to learn how to write good copy. No matter how long it takes.

There is a structure to good sales copy.

The only alternative to writing your own copy would be to hire a professional copywriter but if you don't have the resources for this (good copywriters charge anything from $15,000 upwards) then the only alternative is to do it yourself.

Besides, if you can't recognize good copy from bad copy, then how would you know if what someone has written for you is good or bad?

There is simply no getting around the fact that you have to learn how to write good copy.

The Structure of Good Copy

There is a structure to good copy. I call it "The Anatomy of a Sales Letter."

Take a shufty at the image:

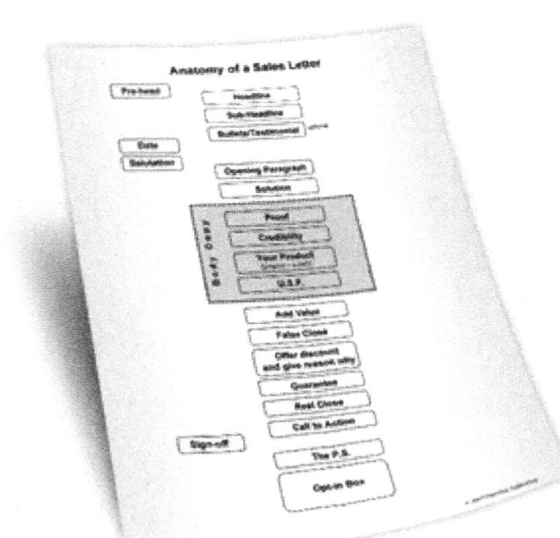

Typically, a basic sales letter has most of the following:

- Headline
- Salutation
- The Lead or Opening Paragraph
- The Problem or Desire
- Agitate the Problem
- The Solution
- Case Studies
- Features and Benefits
- Testimonials
- Guarantee
- Why Buy Today
- Call To Action
- The P.S.s

Sure, there are many variations on the above but the “flow” is generally the same.

In fact, there are some advanced copywriting techniques that don’t follow the above sequence. But this Step is about learning copywriting for beginners so there is no need to complicate or confuse matters.

In this Step, I will stick to the simple order of events, albeit slightly different to that listed above.

Note the title of this Step. It mentions “Persuasive Sales Copy.” That appears to be where most newbies fall down.

This section of this Step is about the structure of your sales copy. And I will amend the basic list above to roughly how I sometimes compose my copy.

Before I list the sequence of events, let's just think about the reader.

Your Ideal Prospect

If you were face to face with your prospect what would you be trying to do?

And what would he be trying to do?

Obviously, you would want to persuade him/or her, to buy your offer. And he would have questions and objections.

You can't just get straight to the point of asking him to buy.

If your sales copy needs to be similar to a one to one meeting with your "ideal prospect" doesn't that mean that your sales copy should be conversational?

Yes, it should.

But it also needs to be more than that.

Your prospect, hopefully your future customer, needs to be taken on a journey. He needs to go from where he is now, to where he wants to be. This is often called a "transformation".

Your prospect wants to get from point A (where he is now), to point B (where he wants to be).

Your sales copy should therefore be written with this in mind.

Much easier said than done.

This technique is a fairly advanced technique but it is also fairly easy to learn. You can write your sales copy in the "usual" fashion and then go over it weaving a "thread" throughout.

I didn't dream up this wonderful prospect journey all on my own, I got it from a guy called Donald Miller, and his book "Building a Story Brand" is on my recommended book list.

His Story Brand technique is just awesome.

The downside being that it is not that easy to blend it into your sales copy. But with a little practice you would get good at it.

So before I try to get that across to you, I will outline one version of how copy is constructed. You'll notice with the diagram just before, that I have sketched this out.

I mentioned a little earlier that when you write your copy you are effectively imagining sat across a table from your prospect. Therefore, doesn't it make sense that you define who your prospect is. What I mean here is your "ideal prospect."

If you can define him (or her), in some detail, then your copy should be written as if it is him/her you are sat across the table from.

Of course, your copy will be seen by hundreds, even thousands of people, but you will write your copy as if they are all average – as is your "ideal prospect"

I acknowledge that it is a little difficult to comprehend at first, but believe me, this simple technique is the recommended way for you to write your copy.

It goes into quite some detail, such as general demographics, profession, earnings etc. The theory being that the better you know your average client, the easier it will be for you to write to just that one person.

You do not write copy to a crowd.

You write to just that one person …

… your ideal prospect.

I don't know what your niche is but we know what niche we have created our offer for – Lost Success Secrets. Below is a shortened version of what my ideal prospect would look like for that niche:

Type	Specific
Gender	• Male
Name	• Chris Taylor (I don't know anyone by this name, I just made that up)
Resides	• Richmond, Virginia, U.S.
Age	• Over 40
Marital Status	• Married 18 years
Children	• Two, aged 8 and 6
Profession	• Engineer
Annual income	• $100,000
Education	• College degree
Social Networking	• Facebook • LinkedIn
Chris' Goals	• Retire early. • Likes the idea of making a passive income online

Chris' Values	• Ethical. • Works hard. • Willing to learn new skills
Chris' Actions To Date	• Has tried many "business opportunities" • Has attended several seminars/workshops
Chris' Challenges	• He feels overwhelmed with what he has tried so far. • He knows what he wants (or thinks he does) but doesn't know how to do it. • Has been led to believe that an online business is easy peasy
Chris' Pain Points	• Has been to several internet-related events and still hasn't achieved an online presence. • He's concerned that his wife may pull the plug on his spending. • He has no plan because nobody has ever explained anything to him. • He has bought product after product but they tend to never get used. • He's frustrated.
Chris' Authority to Purchase	• He is honest with his wife and she is putting pressure on him to stop throwing good money after bad. • He wants to learn and she doesn't understand.
Chris' Objections	• Why should I consider your product? • Nothing's worked for me so far. • I've spent a considerable amount of money and nothing to show for it. • Now you're telling me it's not easy. • I don't know what to believe any more.

There are many more parameters you could insert in there to build an even better, and bigger, picture. But the above list is good to go with.

Sales Copy

In the previous Step I defined an "Irresistible Offer." It turned out to be 4 works in the main offer with 3 bonus works. A neat little bundle of unique and hard-to-find classics.

I mentioned above that when writing sales copy you do not try to sell to a crowd, you are effectively selling to one – your ideal prospect.

And you will construct your copy as if you are actually sat opposite them at a table. In such an environment your ideal prospect would have the opportunity to stop you, ask questions and raise objections.

Therefore, your copy needs to be conversational and all your prospect's questions and objections need to be built in to your copy.

Overall, your copy should tell a story. A story of how your prospect is going to get from where they are now to where they want to be.

You are now in a position to start sketching out your sales copy.

But first … a word of warning!

Writing sales copy is an art and a science. Good copywriters are indeed a rare breed.

It's a funny old world. If you read a piece of (very) successful sales copy, you will almost certainly say to yourself: "Gosh! That was simple. I can do that."

Really? Then just give it a try. I guarantee that you will discover that it is not so easy after all. Good copy looks simple. In fact, good copy is simple. But writing good copy is anything but simple. It takes practice and a hell of a lot of it.

A good copywriter would command a minimum of $15,000 to write copy for you. IF you could get one.

Most of the words in good copy are short and simple. But to put them together is an art form. And the only proof of whether copy is any good or not is not anybody's opinion but the sales that it makes.

Here's what Winston Churchill had to say about short and simple:

"Broadly speaking, the short words are the best, and the old words best of all."

A sales letter either converts or it doesn't.

Remember the equation?

targeted traffic + (a good offer + good copy) = sales

Its now time to examine each element of sales copy:

Some elements are optional or used some times and not other times. The first item is one such parameter:

The Pre-Headline

This is not always used but when it is, it helps to break up what may have been a lengthy headline.

The Main Headline (sometimes referred to as the H1 headline)

This is THE most important part of your copy. Indeed, it is the most important part of your whole marketing process.

The legendary copywriter David Ogilvy said that your headline is 90% of your copy.

Meaning that you should spend 90% of your time writing a sensational headline.

Good, and experienced copywriters, will write one hundred, maybe even two hundred headlines before they settle on the one they want to use.

Best advice: do what the pros do. Write out dozens of headlines until you find the right one.

Ah! But what is the right one?

Answer: you don't know. Nobody knows. In a later Step (#15) you will learn that you have to test, and test again with the intention of incrementally improving your copy. And guess what is the first thing you can test?

You've guessed it. The headline.

It's a fact. If your headline doesn't grab your visitors' attention – you've lost them.

The Sub-Headline

It is recommended that you should use no more than 17 words in a headline.

Now who thought that one up? Nobody. It was discovered with painstaking testing. And in the days before computers.

The pioneers of marketing, guys like John Caples, Claude Hopkins, Rosser Reeves, David Ogilvy, Ted Nicholas, and many others have done a lot of the spade work already – but testing is a never-ending pastime.

Make sure that you do it.

But I'm getting a little ahead here.

If what you want to say in your headline is more than 17 words, then split it up and have a main headline and a sub-headline.

Final word on headlines, for now, is that most visitors to your sales copy will read your headline. The majority of visitors will not read the rest of your copy.

I know, it's sad. But true.

These people are "the skimmers"

To cater for them (and that means most of your visitors) it is good practice to add sub-headlines throughout your copy. That way, even if your visitor just "skims" your copy, he should get the gist of what you are trying to say.

What skimmers are really looking for is the price. More about that later on, but don't make it easy for them.

The basic idea of any headline is to entice your reader to progress further into your sales copy. The writing of headlines takes practice but it can be learned and has to be learned.

There are many "types" of headline but I will outline the most common one here. It is called the "Benefit Headline"

Here is what a good headline should do:

1. Grab the attention of your prospect
2. Promise to solve a problem for your prospect or satisfy any desire he may have

Now is a good time to explain the difference between a “feature” and a “benefit”

Every marketer needs to know this distinction. It is the benefits of a product that will entice your reader to buy.

A feature is something tangible about the product.

A benefit is something that your product can do for your prospect

Good copy is all about benefits and very, very little about features.

Grasp that simple difference and you will be well on your way to writing good copy.

I have devised a simple formula for writing good benefit headlines. But I have to be honest, I didn’t invent the formula, a good friend of mine Phil Gosling was the genius behind it.

But you’re not interested in who devised it, you just want me to give it to you. Right?

Here it is. It has 5 elements, all of which should be in the headline:

- It must contain your biggest benefit
- It must be believable
- It must refer to ease of use
- It must possess a time element
- It will preferably contain some curiosity

To fit all of that into one headline may be difficult. That’s why you could spread it across your pre-headline, your main headline, and your sub-headline.

It wouldn't be fair of me to just leave you with that theory, so here is an example so you can see this formula in action:

I'm a dog lover. But my two dogs are not very obedient so I thought about a product to do with dog training (I've still not gotten around to doing it!) but here's the idea:

"Dog Training" by itself is a fairly big niche, and my little doggies are just that – little. They are teacup Yorkies. So I will settle on: "Yorkie Dog Training" as my niche.

I will imagine that the biggest benefit I want to train them to do is to "fetch my slippers" (and no, I don't have a pipe to go with the slippers 😉)

Following my formula, I'll add some curiosity: how about "the secret command"

And I'll add some believability: "my next door neighbor was amazed"

And finally, I need to state how easy and quickly (ease of use and time element) I could train my little doggies to fetch my slippers.

Or words to that effect.

If I now cobble all that lot together, I come up with a basic headline that looks like:

Main Headline:

"My Next Door Neighbor Was Amazed When My 4 Year-Old Yorkie Fetched My Slippers With Just One Secret Command"

Sub-Headline:

"And You Can Get Your Yorkie To Do The Same And Other Tricks Within 7 Days By Teaching Him Just Twice A Day"

And just so's you get the idea, here's another example. This time the niche is: "Losing Weight"

A major niche, you would not want to be in this niche (it's too large) but this is just an example. The headline is a little coarse, but it can be improved upon later

What's the biggest benefit? "Get Rid of That Spare Tire Without Dieting"

Add some curiosity: "Just By Manipulating Your Tummy"

It must be believable: "Scientifically Proven" (with testimonials and facts to back it up)

How easy is it and how long does it take? "No Equipment Necessary and See Results in Less Than 21 Days"

Now put that all together into a possible sizzling headline and you get:

**"Get Rid of That Spare Tire – Now!
Without Dieting or Exercise Equipment,
Just By Manipulating Your Tummy"**

**"Scientifically Proven Method Will Start
To Show Results in Less Than 21 Days"**

Now, if you are a fat b******* like me, wouldn't that Headline grab your attention? And would you want to read more?

Both those headlines were written literally in 5 minutes. Could they be improved upon? Of course they could. And they should be.

The point being is that they followed the formula.

Did you have any problem knowing what the product might be in the above two examples? I don't think so.

It's surprising how many headlines out there don't give a clue as to what the product is all about. Do not try and be cute with headlines. It rarely works.

I admit, the headlines are a tad on the long side. But do remember, the two examples are but for one type of headline – the benefit headline.

Some of the best headlines in history have been incredibly short. But they are very much the exception.

You could simplify the above headlines. How about a pre-head that says:

Attention! Dog Lovers

Before I get to the opening of the sales copy, sometimes it is proven that Bullets and Testimonials work well at the top of sales copy.

Bullets (or Fascinations) and Testimonials – sometimes referred to as "Deck Copy"

Not always used, but when utilized it can be extremely effective.

Some copywriters like to place a kind of synopsis right at the beginning of their copy. Just under the main headline.

It can work well. Even the skimmers might read them!

And then we come to the sales copy itself.

The Salutation

Tests have proved that your salutation need be no more than: "Dear Friend," you may also feel that "Dear Dog Lover" or "Dear Weight Watcher" is more personal.

Which would you choose?

The answer of course is to test. That'll prove to you which is a clear winner.

Also, it's optional but you could have a mug shot of yourself as part of the salutation.

The Lead (or Opening Paragraph)

Your "Lead" will be crucial.

Remember, the sole aim of your headline is to get your reader to go on and read the next part of your copy.

So it is with your opening few paragraphs.

Your object is to get your visitor to read the next sentence and then the next paragraph, and so on throughout your copy.

Remember also, that 90% of visitors don't read your copy at all. They only consume the headline.

Take a step back and remind yourself what you are trying to do. Your ultimate aim is to sell your product but way before that you must convince your visitor on several things:

- That you are honest

- That you are credible
- That your product will solve their problem or satisfy their desire

Remember also that you have to take your prospect on a journey. Right now, he is at point 'A' but he needs to get to point 'B'

Phew! That's a lot of remembering to do.

And here's another one. Remember what our long lost friend David Ogilvy said about the headline – it is 90% of your copy. Compose a lousy headline and people won't even get this far.

The rest of your copy is the same. Write a lousy opening and people won't read any further.

So you have to start your copy with a big bang and get right in the face of your prospect with his problem.

Play on his emotions.

Remind him that he has a serious problem and that if he doesn't do anything about it, the problem will only get worse. Much worse.

Get him to paint a picture in his mind that it's bad. Very bad. Then get him to picture that it will get horrific if he doesn't act on it.

Then, just as things couldn't get any worse, you give him hope. You present him with a cure for his problem. Which is, of course, your product.

Play to his wants and fears. And then give him a solution.

To give you just a small idea of how this can be done, I'll give you a quick, and simple example.

The niche for this example is: Acne.

I know naff all about Acne, but you can substitute any condition in here:

> Dear Friend,
>
> My name is Spotty Muldoon and I used to live like a recluse. Not very popular. No girlfriends and always ridiculed at school.
>
> Do you, like I used to, suffer from Acne and have had it since childhood? Or maybe it's your child that suffers badly with both spots and their inferiority complex?
>
> Has Acne always held you back? How do you cope with the depression that goes with having Acne? Do you find that having Acne causes you embarrassment when meeting people and talking to people, especially potential partners?
>
> Have you, like I used to, found that with all the over-the-counter prescription treatments, none of them worked?
>
> 'Snot funny is it?
>
> Do you find, that few of these treatments were effective and those that did anything at all – not noticeably so? I thought that if things carried on this way, I would never get rid of my spotty complexion.
>
> I used to get terribly frustrated and locked myself away in my room for hours and hours on end. I used to think that this was it – for the rest of my life – I would never find true friends or a relationship because I was too scared to venture out anywhere.
>
> But then, I discovered that it was not the treatments themselves that I used (although some did work better than others) but the way in which they were applied.

Once I found that out, I cured my Acne in weeks – completely!

Now I lead a very exciting life. Lots of friends, more confidence, and the girls are all over me - like a rash.

Here's my story ... [and continue with the body copy]

Get the idea? Top marketing legend Dan Kennedy had this to say about opening paragraphs:

"Find an itch, scratch it, and then provide a solution."

He must have been thinking about Acne when he said that.

Don't forget – you are writing to small niches and they don't know that all your sales copy follows the same format. Only you know that.

The "problem/make it worse/provide a solution" type of opening can be very powerful. It works.

The Problem (Doom and Gloom)

I've probably covered the problem in the example above but lay it on thick. Really use emotive words and expressions.

Really ram home how serious things are.

As Dan Kennedy said: "Find an itch"

Agitate The Problem (more Doom and Gloom)

Make the reader understand that if he doesn't do anything about his problem it will get worse. Much worse.

And as Dan Kennedy said: "Scratch it"

The Solution (Hope)

Provide your reader with some hope. Then build up to the fact that you have the antidote to his problem.

It is, of course, your product. But you have to build up to the solution.

Body Copy

This phase of your copy is the chunky part.

In this section you will need to provide proof that your solution works. You will need to provide credibility, probably in the form of testimonials. You will need to describe your "irresistible" offer, and you will need to build into your copy your "Unique Selling Proposition" (USP).

If all this sounds a little overwhelming, please hang in there. I will break it all down into bite sized chunks for you.

Composing your sales copy is just about the steepest of learning curves of the whole online business. But as our magic formula proves, you just gotta have it.

Let me, briefly, explain all the salient points.

First up – proof. You need to blend into the story you are telling how the solution that you are proposing worked for you.

It doesn't matter what your offer is all about, people will like you, trust you, and believe you, if you give them proof.

And you need to provide some sort of credibility. Who are you? What is your experience? The best way to do this is to get people that know you and better still, people that have used your products, to give you a testimonial.

If you can garner a testimonial from a well-known person in your niche, that would be very powerful.

Your story needs to get around to talking about your offer. By far the best way to describe your offer is with bullet points. Bullet points are like mini headlines.

Bullets, like headlines, need practice to give them pizazz.

All bullets should be choc full of benefits.

Here are a few examples of how to structure bullets:

- An easy way to …
- A simple, and inexpensive (and little known) tip that will…
- A really cool shortcut to …
- 7 steps to increase …
- 9 simple tricks to …
- How to use …

Study the copy of good marketers, past and present. Guys like Yanik Silver, Joe Sugarman, Matt Furey, Jim Edwards, and many, many more. You will get a ton of great ideas on bullet writing.

Another must to have in your copy is what is commonly known as your "Unique Selling Proposition" or USP. Why are you different? Why are you better? What is it that you do that your competitors don't?

Spy on your competitors. See what they are doing and strive to make your offer better. Your USP might be the price (you are cheaper), it might be your guarantee, whatever it is, make sure you are better in all respects.

A technique that I use is to construct a spreadsheet on my trusty laptop with all the ways that I can be better, or just different, from my competitors. I call this my "Competitive Analysis Spreadsheet".

Competitive Analysis Spreadsheet

Company	#1	#2	#3	#4	#5	#6	#7	#8	#9	#10
Website										
Headline										
USP										
Price										
Offer										
Bonuses										
Guarantee										
P.S.										
Order Form?										
Other Pages										
Up-sell										
Shopping Cart or Clickbank?										
Physical Product or Downloadable?										

Case Studies

If you can produce these you will impress your readership.

Especially if the cases have been a spectacular success. If you can produce these it is advisable to do so. People love to read about others who have made the system work for them. It's something that they can relate to.

Add Value

It's now time to add value to your offer, that is, the description that you place in your sales copy. You know from the previous Step #8 that you do this with Bonuses. But when you are describing them in your copy you don't just say: "…and I've added three bonuses for you, blah, blah, blah"

You not only have to describe your bonuses but also give a reason why you are offering them. Explain to your readers that you really want to make your offer a no-brainer. Explain also that your bonuses cannot be easily found anywhere else, if at all. You did check on your competitors? Yes?

And if your bonuses were to be offered separately (which they could be) they could sell for as much as, or more than, what you are charging for the whole package. Better still, put a value next to each bonus.

The next stage of your sales copy is a technique not widely used, but it is extremely effective. It is called the "False Close".

The False Close

You are now so far into your sales copy, and you have described your offer in quite some detail, your prospect if he has read this far, will be anticipating you to ask for the order.

So you delay this. You change the pace of your copy. Tell a small story. Keep your reader waiting for a small while.

Then, after this minor so-journ, offer your reader a discount, and give a reason why.

Use a phrase similar to:

> *"I was going to charge $197 for this package and it is easily worth every cent of that. Even my colleagues said that I was crazy to even give away any of these secrets at all. But,*

> *quite frankly, it doesn't matter to me how many people know these secrets. They won't affect me.*
>
> *So, I decided to make it really affordable. It's not even $100. You can get your hands on this package for a mere $67.*
>
> *But I may not keep it at that price for long. I may even decide to take the site down altogether.*
>
> *For now though, you can get it all for a measly $67"*

Next, you add your guarantee.

Guarantee

Always, always have a guarantee.

Don't be frightened by people re-funding. If your product is as good as you say it is, you will get few refunds. You will always get some – because there are freebie seekers out there.

The important point is that you MUST give a guarantee and the longer the better.

If you use Clickbank as your payment processor, the guarantee will be fixed by them and at the time of writing this, their guarantee was 56 days.

It is now time in your copy for the real close.

The Real Close

This is where you summarize your offer and ask your readers to buy.

I don't like the words: "Buy" or "Order." People do not logically want to "order" or "buy" anything. But they do want to be sold what they want and that decision is made on their emotions at the time.

They may justify their purchase with logic a little later but at the time of the purchase, the sale is done on emotion.

Preview Section

A good technique after you have asked for the order is to re-cap one more time, your offer. This is called “stacking” and is proven to increase conversions.

You don’t have to do this but it just might help you.

You should try most things. Think of it as just another test. It works or it doesn’t work. You have little to lose. You could have a lot to gain.

Call To Action (CTA)

This is where you actually ask your prospect for the order.

There are two main purposes of a call to action:

1. to tell someone what they should do
2. to give them a reason to do so

I couldn’t believe it either, but if you do not tell your prospect EXACTLY what to do, it is surprising that he will not be able to work it out for himself. So you gotta tell him.

This is usually done visually. I use a CTA button. Like the one just below:

I would also scatter CTA graphics throughout my copy, not all of them looking the same or worded the same. I would vary it somewhat.

The first purpose of a Call To Action is to instruct the prospect to take some kind of action, and in this case it would be to click on the button that says: "Click Here To Reserve Your Place – NOW!"

The second purpose of a Call To Action is to give your prospect a reason to hit the CTA button.

It could be that you have a deadline, for example: "This product is only available for the next 72 Hours"

Or it could play on the psychological trigger of scarcity: "This product will be limited to just 500 copies. When they're gone – they're gone!"

That's fine. Every situation will present its own unique set of circumstances.

I happen to like the psychology of FOMO (the Fear Of Missing Out). The urgency to "order now" plays on the human emotion of not only missing out, but missing out to your competitors.

The wording would go something like: "Get this offer right now before your competitors beat you to it and begin implementing the strategies and stealing your customers from right under your nose!"

Whatever wording you choose to use, you need a strong Call To Action. Ask for the order and give a good reason why they should act NOW.

The P.S.

It is normal to have a Post Script (P.S.) after your signature at the end of your sales copy.

I like to place 3 Post Scripts after my sales copy. But there is one item that you should absolutely NOT have in your P.S.

The price!

As I alluded to earlier, the skimmers will be looking for your price without having to read all your copy. Don't – make it easy for them by putting your price in the P.S.

The Prospect's Journey (The Thread) also called "The Transformation"

I haven't got room in this book to touch upon the technique of weaving a thread throughout your copy. But I like the idea. And you should try to implement it.

It is relatively new but helps the reader feel that he is being taken on a journey from where he is now to where he wants to be.

If your copy is good, he will want to buy it from you.

He is where he is now but he wants to go through a transformation that takes him to where he would like to be.

If your niche is about Acne, he wants to go from being spotty to having an unblemished complexion.

If your niche is Dog Training, he wants to go from having a dog that is dis-obedient to one that obeys your "secret" command.

If your niche is Information Publishing, he wants to go from being broke and knowing very little to being a savvy marketer and living the lifestyle.

Conclusion

This has been an overly long Step and I have still only scratched the surface.

The subject of copywriting is a very special skill. It needs to be learned and it must be learned.

My reckoning is that 99,99% of wannabee marketers that fail do so because their copy is sub-standard. And there is a very good reason of why that is so. People are lazy.

To be able to write decent copy takes time, effort, resources, and plenty of determination.

It's not easy. It requires a lot of persistence.

But the fact is, and there is simply no getting away from it, that without good copy you will be doomed to failure. I can guarantee you that.

I am not a professional copywriter, and nor do I wish to be one. It's a case of horses for courses as far as I am concerned. But I started out by having a mentor and one of the best. Non other than Yanik Silver. If you haven't heard of him then look him up on Google.

I have also partnered with the late, and the great Ted Nicholas.

It was a privilege working with Ted and I learned so much from him. I have read all of his books. I just can't recommend him enough.

I have also partnered with Jim Edwards. Jim is not known as a copywriter but, he's no slouch. His book: "Copywriting Secrets" is one of the best books I have read on the topic. And I have read dozens.

My advice to anyone wanting success on the internet is to get reasonably good at copywriting. The best way to do that is to read and study the topic.

Better still, purchase a course and begin your study there. See my recommended book list at the end of this Step.

I guarantee that with practice you will become a "better-than-average" copywriter if you work at it. If you want success as an information publisher, copywriting will be your key to the kingdom.

Who was it that said: "Just Do It"?

My final word. Copywriters are always asked: "Long copy or short copy?"

It's a common question and there is only one answer. Copy should be as long as it needs to be. Long or short. Write what needs to be written and don't add any fluff. Even non-copywriters recognize bullshit when they see it.

One final point to note on the subject of writing copy is that when you are ready to edit your copy, by all means do so, but let it settle for a day or so.

If you intend to pass it on to a friend or a freelance to edit it then do that also but before you do, here is a brilliant tip: download a copy of the Hemingway app.

www.hemingwayapp.com

What this does is scan your copy and highlight text that is superfluous to requirements. Remember the foregoing text that stated that short words are the best. The Hemingway app picks on this this and suggest that you make the necessary corrections.

Pretty smart, eh?

Your Assignments for Step #9

1. Download the "Anatomy of a Sales Letter" template
2. Use the template you have just downloaded, pin it up next to your place of work and make an outline for your copy.
3. Write at least two dozen headlines (my mentor had me write over one hundred headlines). Partly for practice, mainly for finding the right headline.
4. Practice writing bullets. I would suggest that you write around 100 of these. No kidding. That's what it takes to get good. Bullets need pizazz!
5. Create a Competitive Analysis Spreadsheet and from that decide on your USP
6. Compose a first draft of your sales copy
7. As for good books – there are so many. I have several shelves of books about copywriting. And yes, I have read them all. Some more than once.

But, here is a 'short' list of books I think are good for beginners:

- "Just Get Started" by Ray Edwards
- "Copywriting Secrets" by Jim Edwards
- "Building a Storybrand" by Donald Miller
- "How to Turn Words Into Money" by Ted Nicholas

There are so many good books on copywriting, especially the classics.

8. I would recommend that you invest your time, and resources, into a good copywriting course. There is one that is head and shoulders above all the rest and that is published by the American Writer's Institute titled:

   "Accelerated Program For Six-Figure Copywriting" by Michael Masterson

You can get a copy at: www.CopywritingForSuccess.com

9. The United States is by far the biggest market, and you need to understand their "lingo." Every niche has its own jargon, you'll find all the latest internet speak, and other types of speak in this nigh on 600 page lexicon.

   I therefore recommend that you obtain a copy of: "American Slang" by Robert L. Chapman

10. Finally, grab yourself a copy of the Hemingway app. It's easy to use. And it's free.

This Step and the assignments that go with it, may seem more than a little "weighty" to you. But it is directly proportional to the amount of time and effort that should be given to the subject of writing good copy.

After all, good copy will convert your visitors into buyers. Sub-standard copy will convert all your time and effort into nothing.

Remember, 97% of wannabee marketers fail. Most of them fail because they don't take the trouble to learn how to write good copy. Don't you be one of them.

Step #10

Prepare To Sell More – Increase Your Initial Sale By 40% With This Simple Technique

"Your attitude, not your aptitude, will determine your altitude"

Zig Ziglar

Introduction

This Step is optional, but it is slipped in here because I highly recommend it.

In my early days of information publishing, I hated marketers that used this technique. Whenever I purchased a product, I was always confronted with a: "Before you check out, perhaps you should take a look at our ……" option.

Irritating? Slightly. But does it work? You betcha!

Here is what I mean: at the point of order, that is, your visitor has already purchased your irresistible offer, but right now, before he checks out, you offer him something more.

This is usually a higher-priced offer and related to your main offer.

It may take you more time and effort, because you have to create another product, but it is well worth that extra time.

This technique is commonly known as an "up-sell"

We've all been in McDonald's and the server has said to us: "Would you like fries with that sir?" That's an up-sell.

Or maybe you've been in a restaurant and ordered wine only for the waiter to say: "Large one sir?" That too is an up-sell.

Strictly speaking, an up-sell is when you try to sell an additional product for a higher price.

But of course, it doesn't have to be a higher-priced product, it could be a lower-priced product. In such a case, to be strictly accurate, the sale would then be a "down-sell".

But let's stick to the term "up-sell" for simplicity.

Tests have shown that when people have bought what you are offering, they are already "sold" on what you have to offer.

And because they are already "in the zone" they will be receptive to buying more from you. Statistics have shown that about 40% of buyers of your initial offer will also take you up on your up-sell offer.

The key point here is that this has to be done at the same time as the original purchase – that is, while the prospect still has a bank card in his hand.

Here's how it works:

Your prospect reads your "irresistible offer" and likes what he's just read. He clicks on the "order now" button.

He is then taken to your payment processor (Clickbank) and pays for what he's just ordered, i.e. your main offer.

Now, normally he would be directed to your download page (if your product is a digital one) and download the products onto his hard drive.

But …

If you plan on offering an "up-sell", access to the download page is delayed. What he then sees is an intermediate page that says something like:

"WAIT! Before you download your purchase, you may also be interested in …"

And you proceed to briefly describe the additional product (your up-sell) to him.

Some marketers will have up-sell after up-sell. When I use this up-sell technique I don't have more than one up-sell. Personally, I think it's enough. Others may disagree.

What Makes a Good Up-Sell?

Clearly, any up-sell that you offer has to be related to your niche or complement your offer in some way.

The whole principle of the up-sell is to squeeze as much as you can from a customer that is already "sold".

If your initial product is $47 then a good price point for your up-sell would be something priced at $97.

For the percentage of buyers who opt for your up-sell that means that you have made a sale of $47 + $97 = $144

Tip: get into your mind that online marketing is a numbers game. Once you know your numbers it is simply a case of doing more of what works. Refer to my Special Report on the topic.

For every 1000 visitors you get to your sales page, with a conversion rate of 2%, means you will sell 20 of your initial offer. And 40% of these will go for your up-sell.

Rattle a bit of math and you will make 20 × $47 = $940 but you will also make 8 up-sells at $97 each which equates to 8 × $97 = $776.

Your total sales will therefore be: $940 + $776 = $1716

I think you'd agree, $1716 sounds better than $940

Of course, that's IF your sales copy converts at 2%.

Perhaps now you will be convinced that your sales copy is paramount. It has to be better than good.

What Should Your Strategy Be for Promoting Your Offer

If you were good enough to convert at 2%, or better, how many 1000s of targeted visitors would you want to send to your website? Knowing that for every 1000 you would make an almost clear profit of $1716

Personally, I would be prepared to spend anything up to $2000 to get those 1000 targeted visitors.

"What?" I hear you say. "You'll lose $284 each time. You must be crazy."

Whoah there! No, I'm not crazy. Let me explain ...

In the hypothetical example above, I would gladly spend $284 to acquire 20 new buyers. I also know that I would pick up around 40% of each 1000 visitors as inquisitive prospects. That is, 400 new prospects entering my funnel (see Step #18)

My math was never great at school but I reckon those 20 new customers would cost me $284/20 = $14.20 each.

Wow! Am I some sort of philanthropist or what?

I have acquired 20 new customers and just shy of 400 (four hundred) new prospects. I wonder how many of those 400 I could convert into customers over the next few months!!

What would you call that? I call it list building on steroids.

In my Special Report named: "Know Your Numbers" I highlight several criteria, one of which is called: "The Lifetime Value of a Prospect"

The Lifetime Value of a Prospect is a statistically proven number garnered from your data and it is the amount of money that a loyal customer will spend with you as long as they remain on your lists.

Depending on your niche and the products you create, this figure has been known to be as high as $20,000 and for top, top marketers even higher.

Do you still think I'm crazy?

Maybe your next question will be: "It's all very well in theory, but those numbers you demonstrate look made up."

Really! Made up figures?

They are NOT made up. Ask any successful marketer or refer to other publications and you will find almost identical data.

For now, just accept that it is a numbers game.

What Are Good Examples of Up-Sells?

Back in Step #8 a Front End bundle for a hypothetical product was proposed.

The offer comprised of 4 titles as the main offer, and another 3 works as bonuses, one of which was a PowerPoint summary of 'Think and Grow Rich' by Napoleon Hill.

I would consider that bundle of products "irresistible" and a bargain at anywhere between $47 and $97. The final price being subject to market testing.

It is now time to brainstorm an up-sell product for that niche.

Let us imagine that the original offer is $67 (but could be as high as $97).

I would fancy finding something related to, but very different from the main offer.

I thought and then thought some more and decided to offer as the up-sell a fixed term monthly course.

What I found dove-tailed perfectly with the main offer.

I liked the idea because to offer yet another resource from the Public Domain would, in my humble opinion, be a shade tiresome.

A monthly course was different. Very different.

My research revealed a 17 part course on getting wealthy (a licensed product). Wonderfully written by a guy called Stuart Goldsmith.

My idea was to make available this 17-part course in downloadable format for a price of $27 per month. For those that lasted the whole duration of the 17 months there would be special bonus – as an incentive to stay subscribed.

The special bonus would be free but buyers would need to stay a member of the 17 month course to qualify.

Should buyers last the whole 17 months of the course duration, that up-sell would be worth 17 × $27 = $459

Not bad as a side issue to a low-priced Front End product.

Now if I do the math like before, for every 1000 targeted prospects and with a 2% conversion rate on a $97 offer the figures begin to look extremely magical:

1000 × 2% = 20 buyers

1000 × opt in rate of 40% = 400 prospects

20 buyers × $97 = $1940

8 are attracted by the up-sell: 8 × $459 = $3672 (assuming they stay subscribed for the whole duration)

Total revenue from every 1000 targeted visitors = $1940 + $3672 = $5612

Not too shabby eh?

Not forgetting also that I would have around 400 new prospects to try and convince to buy. Some will and some won't. But the number of buyers will go up – some of those prospects will ultimately buy.

Now, armed with that $5612 and most likely many more from the new prospects still to be converted, how much targeted traffic could you send to your website?

My answer to that question would be that I would invest $6000 to get as much targeted traffic as I could.

With figures like the ones just shown, it is important that your niche is big enough. If you did your research correctly you should have no problem.

Re-investing the proceeds of your sales back into buying more and more targeted traffic is called "scaling" and that is a word you need to make yourself familiar with.

With sales like the ones shown above I would be buying targeted traffic every day of the week and twice on Sundays.

List building on steroids.

Conclusion

For what little extra work it takes to create an up-sell you should do it without any hesitations.

Trust the number testing that has been done by many. Having an up-sell converts about 40% of your normal sale.

You've got absolutely nothing to lose.

But … don't over-do it. We all hate up-sell after up-sell.

Don't pee off your customers. You want to keep them, don't you?

This Step is about "Selling More" and an up-sell is the ideal vehicle to do that.

But your immediate aim should be to ensure that your sales copy converts. Without copy conversion you won't stand a chance. Your whole online publishing business depends on it.

Whatever it takes to get your copy converting is where your efforts need to be right now. In fact, delay adding an up-sell until your copy does convert.

If you are to spend time at this stage, spend it on your copy.

Testing your conversion rate is not dealt with in detail until Step #15. What you have read in this Step are the possibilities of what can be achieved if you add an up-sell to your process.

When you get to Step #15 study it well. Read it in conjunction with my Special Report "Know Your Numbers"

To conclude, you need to understand why you are advised to add an up-sell. If you don't get the why, read this Step again and do some number crunching with your own model. That should convince you.

Your Assignments for Step #10

Two fairly simple assignments for you to conclude this Step.

1. Brainstorm your ideas for an up-sell with a difference. Go to the extent of creating your chosen up-sell and in the next Step (#11) decide whether you want to add it to your site immediately or keep it in abeyance until you have proven your copy conversion.

   Not adding in the next Step will not affect you too much. If anything, it will save you time. But it must be added once you have a satisfactory sales copy conversion rate.

   However, do not make the mistake of thinking that not to add your up-sell in the next Step or wait should not deter you from actually creating your up-sell.

That is your first assignment for this Step.

Just do it!

2. Your second assignment is to get, and read, the following books:
   - "This is Marketing" by Seth Godin
   - "Find Your Why" by Simon Sinek

Step #11

Set Up Your Web Presence Like a Pro Webmaster Using Simple Step-By-Step Instructions That a 10-Year-Old Could Follow

"Websites promote you 24/7: No employee will do that"

Paul Cookson

Introduction

It's at this stage that it is time for you to get everything that you've put together, up on the internet for everyone to see.

You won't get any orders with your offer sat on your hard drive.

You will need to create several web pages, included, but not limited to the following:

- Home page
- Squeeze pages
- Sales page
- Legal page
- Privacy page
- About page
- Contact page
- Order page

- Frequently Asked Questions page
- Customer Capture page
- Intermediate page (for up-sells)
- Download page
- Thank You page
- Opt-in Thank You page

There are many types of software that can build these pages but for beginners I suggest using an easy-to-learn program called Wordpress.

The really good news about Wordpress is that it is FREE! But ...

A word of caution. There are TWO versions of Wordpress. Wordpress.com and Wordpress.org. It is the latter version that you require. The first version is for Wordpress hosted sites, or "hobby" sites as I call them.

Wordpress.org allows you to use your own hosting, which you recall was the subject of Step #6

In that Step it was described how to register a Domain Name and how to set up Web Hosting.

You now need to create the files that will be up-loaded to your hosting company using Wordpress. All the files that you create can then be transferred from your hard drive to the internet, using Wordpress, using a process known as File Transfer Protocol (FTP).

You don't need to know anything about how this is done, Wordpress does it all for you with the press of a button.

Wordpress is a very clever piece of software and is continuously being upgraded.

In its simplest form, Wordpress is basic. However, it can be transformed into a powerful web editing tool by the addition of what are called "plug-ins".

Programmers all over the world are constantly inventing and up-dating plug-ins with the intention of making ordinary websites do extraordinary functions.

The look and feel of websites can also be made to look very professional by the use of what are termed: Themes.

Most plug-ins and themes are free. But the really classy ones are available for modest payments. Programmers have to survive as well.

Types of Web Pages

But before I attempt to give you a simple explanation of Wordpress and its basic functions, I'd like to give a (very) brief description of the various type of web pages, most of which you should have.

1. Squeeze pages (a.k.a. opt-in pages) – if people find you by searching on the internet, they will probably do so by entering a keyword. As you can imagine, your chosen niche will have dozens, even hundreds, of keywords.

   Your potential prospect will "land" on your Squeeze page if the Search Engines show your squeeze page in their results (preferably on the first page).

   Suppose they have searched for "how to be a success" and your squeeze page is optimized for that keyword phrase. Chances are they will find you.

If your squeeze page is optimized for a keyword phrase other than "how to be a success" they will have little chance of finding you.

Doesn't it therefore make sense to have as many squeeze pages as you have keyword phrases so that they can all be optimized for their respective keyword phrases?

Your squeeze pages are also the pages that should have your opt-in process embedded (see also Step #14)

Yes, you understood that right. You will have multiple squeeze (opt-in) pages.

2. Sales page – it might be obvious, but I'll state it anyway. This is the web page where you place your sales message, or copy as I defined it in Step #9

   You only want your sales page to do one thing – sell your offer.

   Web pages are best if they just achieve "one thing" and your sales page should have nothing other than a "Call To Action" or CTA that asks for the sale.

   Your sales page requires no opt-in. Your squeeze pages do all the prospect name collecting

3. Legal page – commonly known as T&C and Disclaimers. Terms and Conditions are commonplace and sometimes referred to as "the small print" but there's no need to get hung up about them. It is possible to find software that can create all the legal pages for you. Similarly, sections such as Earnings Disclaimers are easily found on the internet and easily modelled.

4. Privacy page – your privacy page is another legal document and should be derived from a legal expert.

   It describes how data that you collect about a person will be kept safe from external bodies.

   New laws, such as GDPR need to be complied with and this needs to be stated on your privacy policy.

5. About page – should be written in the 3rd. person, as if someone else is talking about you.

   Your About page is sometimes called a "Bio" page. You need not write pages and pages, but your prospects and customers would like to get to know you

   This page can be about you or your company.

   Place a picture of yourself. Your prospective customers want to see who they are dealing with

6. Contact page – it's not only your prospective customers who might need to contact you, Google like it too.

   There are specific plug-ins that can insert web forms on your contact page (see further down in this Step).

   Set up an eMail address specifically for the Domain name that you have registered.

   Do not use a P.O. Box number for your address. Use a real address where people can get in touch if they feel the need. People like to know that you are indeed a real person.

   You should also add a Google map to your Contact page. This helps not only your visitor but Google love it too.

7. Order page – this page of course will be a synopsis of what you have to offer. Even if your sales page covers your offer in detail, it needs repeating on your order page.

   Everything needs to be clear and concise. Leave your prospect in no doubt as to what is on offer and leave him in no doubt as to what action he should take.

8. Customer Capture page – this is where your new customer signs-up to your offer and is added to your customer list (as opposed to your prospect list)

   You need to keep separate lists. That way you can direct your messages to the right group of people.

9. Intermediate page – this is optional because you would only require this if you were offering an up-sell.

   The idea is that when a buyer of your product is in the process of buying your up-sell as well, he is presented with your intermediate page which describes to him all about your up-sell.

   After he has seen this page, he will be directed to the download page.

10. Download page – this is the page your buyer will see once his transaction has been completed.

    If he declines any up-sell, he will go straight to the download page where he can access the product he has just purchased.

    If he goes for your up-sell, he will first be re-directed to an intermediate page and after completing that, will then be taken to the download page where he can access your main offer and the up-sell.

11. Thank You page – this is the page that is not 100% necessary but it is courteous to do so.

12. Opt-In Thank You page – this page is optional, but again, it is courteous to acknowledge that a prospect has opted-in to receive further information.

13. Frequently Asked Questions (FAQ) page – (optional) prospects and customers have questions and unless you want a barrage of questions on your Contact page, it is generally accepted that having a FAQ page can satisfy all or most of your prospects/customers queries.

14. Blog – to have a Blog is optional but it is a wonderful way of attracting traffic to your website by creating lots and lots of content

15. Getting Started – I hardly see anybody doing this. But I think it is a wonderful idea to guide a new visitor where he needs to go. Don't assume that your visitors know what to do. Most of them need telling what to do.

What is Wordpress?

There are dozens and dozens of website builders available but the most intuitive, cheapest, and easiest to use, in my opinion, is the self-hosted Wordpress platform.

It is not just my opinion, Wordpress is also the most popular, it powers more than one third of the top ten million websites connected to the internet.

Are there better website builders available? Of course there are. But most of them cost money because of their high development costs. Programs such as Dreamweaver, Joomla, Shopify, Drupal, Weebly, Wix, etc.

Wordpress was developed as a blog platform but is now used by beginner marketers. Some experienced marketers still use Wordpress. As do some large corporations – eBay, CNN, Ford, UPS, Reuters, Forbes, Sony, the list goes on.

There are two versions of Wordpress. Wordpress.com and Wordpress.org.

You will need the latter. Wordpress.com is for people with hobbies and the hosting and domain are taken care of for you.

You will need to install Wordpress.org on your website using your own Domain name and your own hosting.

Wordpress.org is still free. It is called "Open Source" and is easy, stable (robust) and flexible.

In this expensive world in which we live, it's really refreshing to find something as big and as useful as a fully functional web site builder to be available for zilch, nada, nichts.

True, if you want to make your Wordpress website into some all-singing, all-dancing affair you may have to pay to get premium plug-ins and a premium theme (explained later). But for a basic website that gets the job done – it needn't cost you a dime.

Your only expense will be to register a domain name and set up hosting – which you have already done in Step #6

The eMail you will have received from your hosting company will give you details of how to access your control panel, or cPanel as it is known.

Your hosting dashboard, not to be confused with your Wordpress dashboard (see next section), is where you can set up eMails and most importantly where you will install Wordpress.

Installing Wordpress

When you get into Wordpress' cPanel you will notice lots of icons. Don't get frustrated. Most of them you will never need.

Look for the blue icon with the Wordpress logo that is titled "Install Wordpress"

It's self-intuitive.

You will be prompted to choose a 'protocol'. Enter: http://

Then a domain name. Enter: your domain

In the 'directory' box, delete the pre-filled 'wp' entry and leave the box empty. If you don't do this your website will be installed in a sub-folder which is not what you want.

You will be asked to enter an admin username, and a password (you can change any of these later if you so choose but make it a strong password).

Check all the other options and press "install"

You do not need to install anything else at this stage. The task in hand right now is to get Wordpress installed on your website.

Once installation has completed you will be taken to a screen with your Wordpress login URL and password.

That's it! Congratulations.

You have just created your first Wordpress website.

You can now schlepp on over to your Wordpress login page.

Your login URL will take the form:

http://www.yourdomain.com/wp-admin

Now login with the username and password you created earlier (and make sure that you save your username and password in your little book).

Before going any further, it's a good idea to get a little familiar with the 'Wordpress Dashboard'

If you get stuck, like I still do from time to time, YouTube is very useful for short, specific tutorials on all things Wordpress.

The Wordpress Dashboard

When you first log in to Wordpress you are presented with the Dashboard.

It will have the following components:

- Dashboard 'homepage'
- Posts
- Media
- Pages
- Comments
- Appearance
- Plugins

- Users
- Tools
- Settings

Each of the above would have a drop-down box revealing further options.

A Typical Webpage

A typical webpage would have some, or all of the following:

- Headline
- Menu(s)
- Contact
- Sidebar
- Footer

Essential Plug-Ins

I reckon you want to know: what is a "plug-in"?

A fair question. When I first started out building websites with Wordpress, people used to talk this foreign language called Wordpress jargon. I didn't have a clue what they were on about.

But I made it my business to find out. I didn't know what they meant when they talked about plug-ins, themes, widgets and other stuff.

A Plug-in is a piece of software that can be added to a Wordpress website. It can add functionality to the website without the user knowing a single thing about code.

Basically, Wordpress is not much use without any plug-ins. It is the variety of plug-ins that make Wordpress as popular as it is today. It is estimated that there are over 60,000 plug-ins available for Wordpress. Some free. Some paid for.

However, you will only need something like 10-20 of them

Plug-ins can do all manner of things. For example there are plug-ins that can:

- Speed up your website
- Optimize your website for Google
- Back up your website
- Secure your website from hackers
- Add a simple or a complex contact form
- Offer your visitors a way to share your content on their Social Media channels
- Split test web pages for conversion
- Create price comparisons
- Manage and track the links on your website
- Automatically link internal pages on your website

Now here's the rub: there are some essential plug-ins that you must install. There are also plug-ins that are "nice-to-have". Here's a list of what I install on my websites:

1. Akismet – anti-spam filter
2. Yoast SEO – the number one website optimizer
3. WP Insert – installs Legal Pages for your website

4. Yoast XML Sitemap – makes it easier for the search engines to track your web pages
5. Updraft Plus – backs up your files and database
6. WP Forms - can manage multiple contact forms, plus you can customize the form and the mail content. Google Maps is a useful addition to contact forms.
7. Google Analytics by Yoast - gives you step-by-step instructions on how to find data that will help you track your SEO using Google Analytics
8. All In One WP Security and Firewall - WordPress is already a very secure platform, but it also helps to add some extra security and firewall to your site
9. WP Super Cache - increases website performance and reduces loading times
10. Paypal Shopping Cart or Woo Commerce – these are online payment options to offer your customers

It is recommended to have no more than 20 plug-ins installed on your website. Too many could slow down and de-stabilize your website.

Plug-ins can be added and managed from the Wordpress admin area via the dashboard by selecting: Plugins >> Add New

The Look and Feel of Your Website

The 'Look and Feel' of your website is controlled by what is called a 'Theme'.

I know what you're thinking: "What the heck is a Theme?"

A 'Theme' is a template and stylesheet used to define the appearance and display of a Wordpress website.

Nobody likes to look at an ugly website.

There are almost as many themes available as there are plug-ins. Some are free, some to pay for. The big difference between plug-ins and themes is that once you have made your choice of theme – you only need that one.

Wordpress has its own library of Themes from which to choose from in their Theme Directory.

However, as information publishers we will be marketing our offer via a sales page. Ref: Step #9 and as such we will require a sales page specific theme.

All of my websites are sales page oriented and it took me an age to figure out what theme to use, and despite asking many marketers. I was directed to all manner of options, nothing was really suitable. Until ...

Master marketer Armand Morin gave me the solution.

Armand has an answer to everything, and in this case, it was an easy answer for him because he has designed his own theme specifically for information marketers.

It's easy when you know how. Here is the link to his sale letter theme:

https://wpsalesletter.com/

Themes can be added and managed from the Wordpress admin area via the dashboard by selecting: Appearance >> Themes

Another useful theme is: Astra.

You can play around with themes. Even if your content is already done you can change from one theme to another with little, or no visible problem.

The Block Editor

This Step just would not be complete without a brief mention of the latest addition to the Wordpress family – the Block Editor.

Up until quite recently, you had to edit pages within Wordpress by what was known as a classical editor. Very similar to how Microsoft Word is edited.

But Wordpress, in their wisdom, have come up with a new innovation (Wordpress 5.0) that uses blocks to edit pages.

You can still use the "old" classical editor by installing a plug-in, but why would you want to do that? The Block Editor is now the way to go – although it has been found that some themes do not work well with the new editor. Teething problems I'm sure.

The new Block Editor treats all of your content as individual blocks.

Each block can be inserted, re-arranged, and styled individually thus making this new innovation much more flexible than the old classical editor.

You can add blocks for paragraphs, headings, ordered and un-ordered lists, quotes, images, buttons, tables, columns, and much, much more.

The Block Editor allows you to drag and drop in order to re-arrange the order of individual blocks

Conclusion

Wordpress is a simple program and simple to install.

However, simple does not always mean “easy”. But 65 million website owners can’t be wrong.

There can be some intricate stages when both installing and using Wordpress. I recommend both a good book and a good online course for your better understanding.

If you are in any doubt whatsoever about installing Wordpress, then outsourcing is another option for you. If you do choose this option, I would recommend trying to get someone local to you.

If you feel confident in doing it yourself – well done.

I’m no techno genius but I just about got it done, but being honest, it took a lot of my time. It’s like most things in life, the more you play with it, the better you will become.

This Step can only scratch the surface. But you should be able to install Wordpress on a host of your choice, using your own domain, and be able to set up the most rudimentary of websites.

A Wordpress site is secure and responsive, that means mobile friendly. Mobile users are very quickly becoming mass users.

My advice for any would-be online information publisher is to get ultra-familiar with Wordpress. It is now the industry standard and is only going to get better and better.

Make your life easy – go with a winning trend, and that trend is Wordpress.

Your Assignments for Step #11

No prizes for guessing what your assignments are for this Step.

1. Understand the content of this Step in detail. Go out of your way to find out as much about Wordpress as you can. By all means get a webmaster to set up your website but understand everything that he has done.

   You do not want to be reliant on some webmaster holding you to ransom. Get to know how to build, and maintain your own website. It will come with practice - it did for me.

2. Install Wordpress on your web host. Study the Dashboard and get to know all of its functions. If you get stuck ask for help, or see 3. below.

3. My number one recommendation is that you do two things:

   a) Get yourself a copy of Dr. Andy Williams' book: "Wordpress for Beginners 2020: A Visual Step-By-Step Guide To Mastering Wordpress"

   b) Dr. Williams also has a Udemy online course titled: "Wordpress For Beginners: Master Wordpress Quickly" It is very reasonably priced at around $15

I suggest you obtain, and devour, both resources. For sure, you will then know more than most webmasters.

Dr. Williams is an ex-teacher and knows how to get a point across. He is a man worth following.

4. A fantastic source of free information can be found on YouTube.

   You will find videos that take you through the whole process of installing Wordpress or there are videos that explain specific steps.

   YouTube is a tremendous resource. Use it.

Step #12

Set Up Your Order Taking Process

"Fall in love with the process, and the results will come"

Anon

Introduction

There are several ways in which you can set up your order-taking process but one of the simplest is what I will describe here.

The name of the order taking system is called "Clickbank."

It is extremely easy to use and extremely cost effective. It's not free, but it doesn't cost the earth either.

Setting up a Clickbank account will cost you a one-off fee of $49 (at the time of writing).

When you make a sale from your website, Clickbank will process that sale for you and make regular payments to you by cheque or make payments directly into a bank account of your choice.

One BIG advantage I really like about Clickbank is their army of affiliates.

If you don't know what an affiliate is, they are your fellow marketers who will find your offer in the Clickbank Marketplace, and if they like it, they will promote it to their existing customers.

This is really advantageous for you as you will make sales that you would not normally make. Of course, you will have to pay these affiliates a commission (usually 50% but can be more) but you will also get the added benefit of another customer and perhaps several prospects.

As you accumulate customers and prospects you must build a relationship with them. Your customers and your prospective customers will be the lifeblood of your online publishing business.

Step #14 will elaborate on how you can do this.

For this Step, you will understand how your new customers will be able to access their new purchases.

The Sales Process

The Sales Copy that you composed in Step #9 would have included some form of 'Call To Action' or CTA as it is abbreviated to.

This Call To Action would normally be in the form of an 'order' button, although you would never name your CTA with the words 'order' or 'buy'.

A much better alternative would be 'Reserve Your Copy Now' or 'Register Me Now'

When you get to Steps #15 and #17 your CTA is something that you can test. Only then would you find out which CTA works the best.

Sub-consciously, people don't like to think that they are 'buying' something, but of course that is exactly what they will be doing.

CTAs that have worked best for me have been in graphical form. See the example below:

I can't design graphics for the life of me. It is one (of many) tasks that I have to outsource. There are many places you can outsource (see Step #7) I have had good service using:

www.OnlineJobs.ph

You will observe, that nowhere on the graphic does it use the words: 'order' or 'buy'

When your prospective customer clicks on your 'order' button, he will be directed to your order taking process.

I use three different order taking methods, I will describe one here with a cursory mention of one of the others. As a publisher of purely digital products this one method should serve you well.

For your information, the three order taking process methods that I use are:

- Total Business System Shopping Cart
- Clickbank
- Paypal

The very next section I will describe Clickbank and mention Paypal briefly because it is so popular.

Opening a Clickbank Account

Clickbank is a perfect solution if you want a simple, easy-to-learn, and quick system.

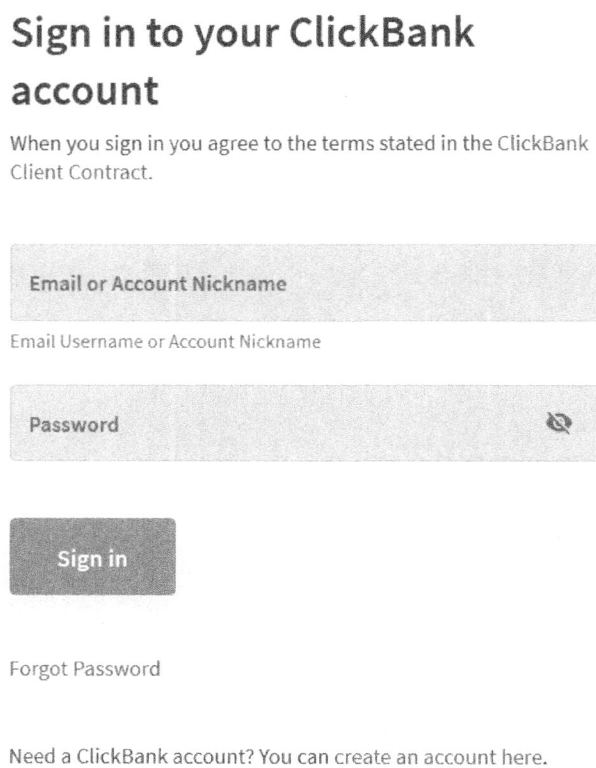

The beauty of Clickbank is that it handles everything. It takes your payments, processes your order, and even handles affiliates.

It's a one-stop shop. Especially for beginner marketers.

My recommendation is that you start with downloadable (i.e. digital) products.

As a seller of a product, which is what you will want to be, log into Clickbank and go to the tab marked: "sell products" and complete the sign-up process.

The Clickbank sign-up form is self-explanatory. You will be asked for a "nickname" Make sure that what you choose is memorable and don't forget to enter this into your password book. Remember? The one you acquired in Step #6

During the sign-up process, Clickbank will eMail you a password, or 'confirmation code' as they call it.

Make sure you enter this into your password book as well.

Once logged in look for a tab titled: "Vendor Settings" and then "My Products"

You will then be given options on a range of different type of products for you to promote. You need to choose: "Standard Product"

Next, select "Add New: Product" and a drop down box will appear with options for:

- Physical Products
- Digital Products
- Hybrid Products i.e. Physical and Digital

Choose: "Digital Products" and "one time digital product"

You will be taken to an intuitive "Create a New Product" page

It is on this page that you will also:

- Set your price
- Name your "Pitch" page
- Name your "Thank You" page
- Upload your product.

As a first time customer of Clickbank, they will insist on approving you. Don't be scared of that, it is all done on this same "Create a New Product" page.

There is something that you need to be aware of regarding your "Thank You" page. If you simply call it "ThankYou.html" it will be too easy for people to guess, and, possibly hack into your website and get your product for free.

Here's what I do. I create a separate folder for my websites and name it something nobody could easily guess. Something like: "shbympapw" – nobody but me knows what that means and it's hardly guessable.

Then I create my "Thank You" page within that folder. For example:

https://www.YourDomain.com/shbympapw/
download_page_for_Customer.html

Even with the html extension I make, it difficult to guess what it is. Note the upper and lower case spelling!

The "Title" that you enter can be simply your Domain name but I prefer to add a little more. Something like: Your Domain Name – Make 60% on Every Sale.

The reason I do this is because when you list your product in the Clickbank Marketplace, not only will buyers be looking for your product, but potential affiliates will be looking as well. Therefore, make the second part of your title a benefit statement to attract affiliates.

When you are happy with your entries, hit: "Save Changes"

You will then be taken to a revised "My Products" page where you can see all the details you just entered, and showing a status of "Pending Approval Request"

Clickbank will not approve your product until they see your complete sales process. Which means that your sales copy has to be finished and your web presence established.

There is a one-time cost of $49 to be paid to Clickbank. After this payment, Clickbank make a charge of $7.50 + $1 for every transaction thereafter. A tad pricey, but Clickbank is a first rate company and has been around a long time.

Clickbank is now a slick website. It used to be a little cumbersome. There are now lots of places to get help on their site. And the big change I think is that they now accept physical products.

Integrating Paypal Into Your Sales Process

Use Paypal as an additional payment option rather than as an alternative option.

Not everyone has a Paypal account. But a lot of people that do, like to use Paypal for their purchases. So you should make it easy for them.

For some reason, a lot of people don't view money in their Paypal account as "real money"

Not everyone has a credit card either, so having a Paypal as an option in your order process will catch these buyers. Try to cater for everyone.

Of course, to offer Paypal as an option, you will require a Paypal account yourself. If you haven't already got one, well, you know what to do!

Go to: www.PayPal.com

Conclusion

This is a major Step. After all is said and done, you want to be paid don't you?

There are many payment options in the market place, I just recommend Clickbank and Paypal for their simplicity.

Having said that, Clickbank has had to "up its game" in this last few years and what a great job they have done.

There isn't much you cannot do now with Clickbank – they can handle payments for digital products, physical products, or a combination of the two, part payments and also recurring payments.

As an information publisher there's not much more that you would need.

I have no hesitation in using Clickbank and neither should you. They have been around since 1998. It is an ideal platform for online information publishers like ourselves.

It is prudent to offer Paypal as a secondary method. You do not want to be excluding anybody.

Your Assignments for Step #12

No let up.

Plenty for you to do this Step. But, as always, break everything down into bite-sized chunks and they don't seem half as difficult – do they?

Your task(s) then for this Step are:

1. Sign up for Clickbank. You will require your sales copy and web presence complete to be able to do so
2. Get ultra-familiar with Clickbank by devouring everything on their shiny-new website.
3. Have a good poke around the Clickbank Marketplace, it may give you some inspiration
4. Sign up for a Paypal account if you haven't already got one.
5. Get, and read: "Wordpress Magazine: Paypal Shopping Cart and SEO" by Sunny Chanday

Step #13

The Money's In The Marketing – The Marketing of Your Offer Will Determine Your Success Or Failure

"If content is king, then conversion is queen."

John Munsell

Introduction

Phew! Step #13 already. You're not superstitious are you?

I hope not, because this Step is where the rubber really hits the road.

Internet marketing or information marketing are aptly named.

The key word is "marketing"

Nothing happens until you make it happen but if you have done all the Steps leading up to this one, you will be in good shape for what is to come.

You should by now have a website that is on the World Wide Web for all to see. Except that people will not be able to see your website unless you tell them it's there.

It's analogous to having a bricks and mortar business which is located in a quiet part of town. If you don't do some advertising – nobody will know that you are there.

This Step is an introduction to the world of marketing. Mostly online marketing.

However, the techniques described here should not be put into practice until you have successfully completed Step #15

This Step is an overview of online marketing.

The Basics

Before you can even think about doing any marketing, you must grasp a very basic principle. A principle that is best explained with my favourite little piece of arithmetic. You've seen it before:

Traffic + conversion = sales

It doesn't get much simpler than that.

But if it's so simple, why do most people fail? And they do fail.

We all know that the ultimate aim of any business is sales, but, according to our magic formula above, we can't make sales until we have two other components in place.

And from this point on, it isn't that simple any more. It is, after all, where the majority of people fail.

So I'm saying to you right now, that you need to get that formula ingrained into your mind. In fact, I like to modify it – albeit ever so slightly.

Highly targeted traffic + conversion = sales

That revised formula is the first clue as to why most people fail.

They know that they need visitors to their website but they send the wrong type of visitor. It's a common problem.

But it ain't the biggest problem.

The biggest problem, by a country mile, is the conversion element of that formula.

What does conversion mean?

That's a great question and it deserves a great answer.

Before I attempt to answer, I must state that failure to convert is the most likely reason 97% fail in online marketing. I'm sure that you'll agree that this is an extremely high percentage.

In Step #9 you should have completed your "Conversion Piece" I only call it that because it fits in with the magic formula. It is, of course, your Sales Copy.

Conversion means the ability of your Sales Copy in "converting" your visitor from a prospect, into a buyer. To repeat - 97% of websites fail to convert.

You will find out in Step #15 whether your copy will convert or not.

I can tell you right now, if you have just glossed over Step #9 (Compose Your Conversion Piece) you will be a member of the 97% club. Of that, I am 100% certain.

Of all the Steps in this book, and of all the Steps in any book on marketing, and of all the Steps in any marketing course, the section on writing copy is THE most important step of them all.

It's not even up for discussion. You must have sales copy that converts. End of story.

To sum up this section, to have any chance of making sales you need two vital components:

1. Highly targeted visitors
2. Sale copy that converts

Sounds easy enough. But ...

Most people fail. They fail because of the two reasons above.

I'll make a BIG assumption now, I will assume that you have got the two elements of the magic formula all sorted. Time to move on to the next stage, which is:

Building Traffic

Building your own lists is the best way of building traffic.

I will assume that you are starting a new online information publishing business and have no lists whatsoever.

In the next Step (#14) I go into more detail about building your lists. This section is just a brief introduction.

You will hear people all the time stating that "your list" is the most important thing. That's only about one third correct.

It is the "relationship" that you have with your lists that's important.

It is also a list of "buyers" that you need to build as quickly as possible.

Building your own lists is definitely important to your success. If you possess a sizeable list of buyers, that is a free source of highly targeted visitors to any of your websites.

I mention in the next Step that there are only three kinds of traffic:

- Traffic that you Build
- Traffic that you Buy

- Traffic that you Borrow

You will use all three but by far the cheapest is the traffic that you build. It's obvious isn't it? Your lists belong to you. They are yours, and yours only to market to.

The sooner you start to build your lists the better.

You will also discover in Step #14 that you will build lists. That is more than one list.

As a minimum, you will build a prospect list – the people who "opt-in" and receive your "ethical bribe". Secondly, you will build a customer list – the people who buy your product.

In fact, you will have several versions of each list depending how many products you ultimately have.

Now here's a funny thing.

You will discover later that when you try to market your product, only a very small percentage will either opt-in to find out more or, actually convert to buyers.

That very small percentage is in the zero to a few percentage points: 1%, 2%, or 3% if you're lucky.

But "wait a mo!" I hear you cry, "I have supposedly sent 'highly targeted traffic' to my website, why have only a few visitors opted-in (perhaps 20%) and a lot fewer actually bought my product, i.e. became customers (1% or 2% even)?"

"That doesn't sound like 'highly targeted traffic' to me."

That is a great point and I cannot give you any great answer except: "that's just the way it is."

A friend and mentor of mine, Armand Morin, has a partial answer to this quandary. He creates multiple opt-in pages. He calls it his '30X Principle'

He literally creates a separate opt-in page for every keyword that his target market may use. Yes, he may create 30 different opt-ins. Some of his students have created hundreds of opt-in pages.

That's a way of getting your opt-in percentage higher and your prospect list greater.

And here's little tip for building your buyer list.

In the next Step I talk about your buyer list being the list of people who have bought your products and the number that do buy determine your percentage conversion rate.

However, you will want to build your buyer list as fast and as big as possible and if your first product is priced at say, $97, there will be people that view your offer, and no matter how irresistible it may be, they will not be prepared to part with $97.

Here's what some marketers do in order to build their lists fast.

Self Liquidating Offers (SLO)

They sacrifice time initially and build a really low-priced product. They may have already created a "free" ethical bribe to tempt their readers to opt-in but sometimes they create a valuable opt-in product and charge a "small" fee instead of giving it away for free.

This in marketing is generally known as a: "self liquidating offer."

Who thought that name up you might ask?

This has generally worked well for me too.

Think about it. If people are indisposed to spend $97 on a product, for whatever reason, they will generally not baulk at spending a fraction of that. I would generally keep the price of this "offer" under $10

Psychologically what this does is sought out the men from the boys. The freebie-seekers from the serious.

If you try this you might just find that your conversion rates will not be as good as your prospect opt-in rate but they will almost certainly be infinitely better than the miserly 1% and 2%. I have achieved over 40% opt-in rates using this technique and a 20% conversion rate.

Not a bad way to build your lists.

The downside is: it is another product for you to create.

The goal of a self liquidating offer is to recover your ad costs.

Let me explain:

You want to build your lists fast. But you have two kind of lists: prospects and buyers. Prospects are those visitors that have not bought from you yet, and buyers are those that have bought from you.

Here's a question: "Would you rather have a list of buyers or a list of prospects?"

Yes, I thought that you'd choose buyers.

However, most people will not want to part with their hard-earned easily but for a product priced under $10 they would not think twice. It's pocket change to them.

I know this works because I've done it several times.

Say you offer a SLO for $7 and out of 1000 highly targeted visitors you sell 100 (a conversion rate of 10% - which is actually on the low side) that means you will have raked in $700. Which in turn means that you could afford to spend $700 on advertising to drive those 1000 visitors to your website.

Why wouldn't you do this?

And where would you get your $7 product from?

Also, don't forget, that out of those 1000 visitors you have accumulated 100 new customers, but you will have acquired 400 new prospects as well (assuming that your prospect opt-in rate remains at 40%)

I don't know why marketers don't use this technique more often. I don't know why I don't use it more often.

List Building is my favorite way of building traffic.

Other Ways to Build Traffic

Other sources of building traffic are:

- Search Engine Listings
- Your own eZine
- Linking Strategies
- Social Networking

- Blogs
- Article Submission

All of the above are beyond the scope of this book but just recognize the potential that there is in each one of these.

The next method of acquiring traffic is buying traffic.

Buying Traffic

By far my favorite method of buying traffic is by using Pay-Per-Click or PPC as it is generally referred to.

I'll not go into the ins and outs of how to do this, it is mentioned in more detail in future Steps.

I like PPC because it is instant traffic. And if you get ultra-familiar with PPC, you will find that it is not that expensive (see the examples in future Steps).

People that whinge about PPC are the ones that have not taken the trouble to understand it. They have only themselves to blame. But of course, they won't do that, will they?

My favored PPC supplier is Google Ads (formerly known as Adwords). Their system has been super-efficient since it was launched in the early 2000s.

There are other PPC advertisers notably:

- Facebook
- LinkedIn
- YouTube
- Pinterest
- Twitter

And other sources of buying traffic are:

- Classified Advertising
- Banner Advertising
- eZine Advertising
- Direct Mail

The next few Steps of this book, go into PPC advertising in greater detail.

The next method for acquiring traffic is to borrow from other marketers:

Borrowing Traffic

Partnering, or Joint Venturing (JV) with other established marketers, is what goes on every day.

Many marketers in the online information publishing business like this option. It can give your project a real boost.

The obvious downside being that you have to share the revenue from any sales made. This is usually 50%.

But before you say: “How much?” let me explain:

You are a beginner. You have no list of your own – yet. And you don’t want to spend an arm and a leg on pay-per-click advertising until you have some money coming in.

Take the following scenario …you are attending a seminar one week-end and get talking to one of the speakers who offers to do a mailing of your offer to his list of 100,000 customers. The recognized split is 50:50 as mentioned earlier.

Are you going to say: “yes” or “yes” to his offer?

Fair enough. You have to forfeit half of the revenue that accrues from his mailing.

Let's say his list likes your offer and it achieves a 3% conversion. That would be 3% of 100,000. My trusty calculator reckons that to be 3,000 sales.

Crikey! If your product is a $97 product that's 3,000 x $97 = $291,000. Under your terms of your agreement with him, he would get $145,500 and you would receive $145,500

Would that have been worth the trip to travelling half way around the world?

N.B. Big players in your niche are not that interested in low-priced products. 50% of $37 is not worth their while. The pricier the better as far as they are concerned.

Don't for one minute think that is pie in the sky. It happens.

You cannot think: "Shucks, I have to give away half of my revenue." You have to think: "any revenue I get from this deal is money that I would never have made otherwise."

And don't forget too, that an added benefit of working with a JV Partner is that you build your list too. In the above example you just acquired 3,000 more customers and probably around 15,000-20,000 prospects.

Not bad for a chance meeting.

Very similar to Joint Ventures is Affiliate Marketing.

It is one of the main reasons that I choose Clickbank to be my preferred option as a payment processor. They have an in-built affiliate network – called the Clickbank Marketplace.

Convert well and affiliates will be beating a path to your door. You will start making sales from nowhere.

Other sources of borrowing traffic are:

- Affiliate marketing
- Other Peoples' Blogs

Conclusion

Internet marketing.

That's the clue, your success will be determined by how good your marketing is.

And your marketing will get a really good start if you get the magic formula committed to memory.

Highly targeted traffic + sales copy conversion = sales

As long as your sales copy converts and you send highly targeted traffic to your website, you can't help but make sales.

Getting highly targeted traffic is not rocket science. If you have chosen your niche wisely, there will be plenty of targeted traffic for you.

Once your sales copy converts at anything above 1% switch on those traffic faucets and just watch the sales roll in. You won't be able to stop it.

Spend the time NOW to get these basics right and your future will be rosy.

I have listed nearly 40 methods of driving traffic to your website (see Step #16), get good at say, 6 of them and outsource the rest.

Marketing is a numbers game.

Keep the 'Magic Formula' in your mind. It just can't fail.

Master marketers have known this for years. They know that when they market to their lists what return they expect.

Every top marketer that I know, and I do know quite a few, are no slouches when it comes to writing persuasive sales copy.

Just like the pioneer marketers before them, they made it their business to be good at sales copy.

All top marketers also know about the importance of highly targeted traffic.

Combining highly targeted visitors and good persuasive copy is a "just can't fail" combination.

They know it – and now you know it.

Your Assignments for Step #13

This is the point when you need to start thinking seriously about income.

It is the marketing that you do that will determine your success.

Your assignment(s) for this Step are:

1. Commit to memory the 'Magic Formula'
2. You must use all three methods of obtaining traffic and then pick at least one technique from each.

   Pick at least one technique from each method:

   - Building Traffic

     a) Your own lists

   b) SEO
   c) Facebook
   d) LinkedIn

- Buying Traffic
   a) Google Ads
   b) Facebook Ads
   c) LinkedIn Ads
- Borrowing Traffic
   a) Joint Venture Partners (JVs)
   b) Affiliate Networks e.g. Clickbank

3. Get, and read, the following books:
   - “The Ultimate Marketing Plan” by Dan Kennedy
   - “The 1-Page Marketing Plan” by Allan Dib
   - “The Tipping Point” by Malcolm Gladwell

Any book by Dan Kennedy on marketing is worthy reading.

Reading alone, will not make you successful – but no reading at all will guarantee your non success

Step #14

Build a Relationship With Your Lists and Sell To Them Over and Over Again

"If you aren't building your list you are missing out on the future of your business"

Vicki Fitch

Introduction

Quite frankly, it is never too soon to start building your lists.

What I have tried to do with these Steps is to present each activity in a logical order.

With that in mind I have positioned this Step directly after you have begun to acquire customers.

In practice, you will build a minimum of two lists. One for prospects (i.e. prospective customers) and a list for actual customers.

You could start building your prospect list from the very beginning. One way to do this would be via your LinkedIn page and other Social Media sites.

A list of customers, that is, people who have opened their wallets and put their faith in you by buying your offer, is like gold dust. If they like what you have sold to them, there is a very good chance that they will buy from you again.

Doesn't it make sense that you should treat them with a lot of respect?

Of course it does.

And what about the people who haven't bought from you (yet) but also arrived on your website to "take a look"? These are known as prospects.

Prospects or Customers, you will need a means of collecting their name and primary eMail address in order that you may contact them in the future.

For this you will require a piece of software that automatically collects the full name and primary eMail address of your prospects and your customers.

The system I use and suggest that you do too is called:

Total Business System

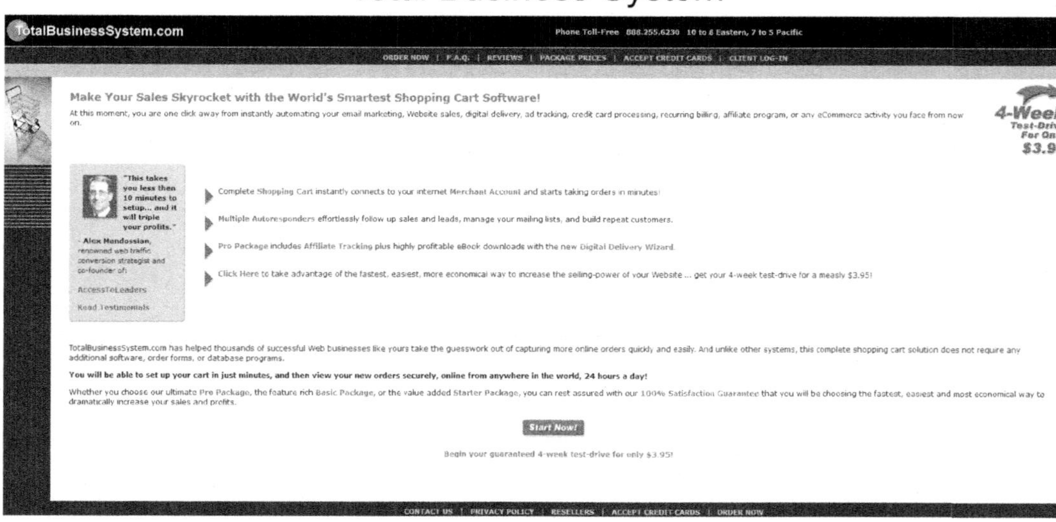

Total Business System does a lot more than just collect names and eMails, it is a complete e-Commerce system. Think of it as an online Shopping Cart.

But you will only need the eMail capabilities of the software.

Auto-Responders and Broadcasts are all that you will require (see below for a more detailed definition).

No worthwhile software is free but Total Business System is extremely cost effective and a reliable list building tool. It is a necessary business expense and at only $34 per month the cost is minimal.

Total Business System is fully Can-Spam compliant, allows you to run your own e-zine or newsletter, has online tutorials, and offers full support.

You can access the website at:

www.TotalBusinessSystem.com

Web Form or Custom Form

A Web Form or Custom Form is just another name for the form that you need to create for collecting prospect or customer data.

With Total Business System it is easy to create a web form.

From the "eMail and Marketing" drop down menu select: 'Web Forms' and then select 'Create New'

You will see something like the screenshot below:

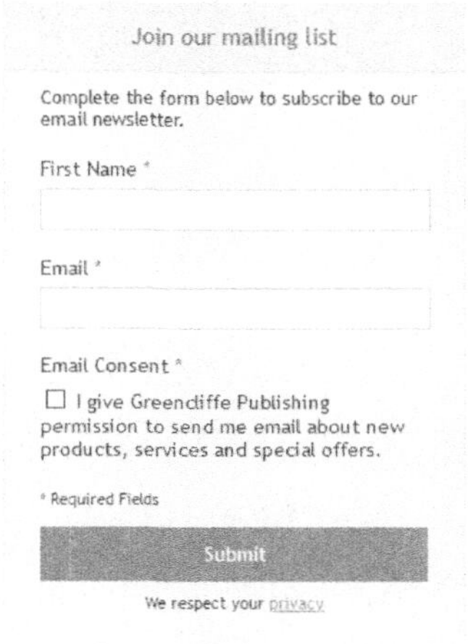

The html code that you obtain then needs to be copied and pasted into your squeeze page. See the screenshot below:

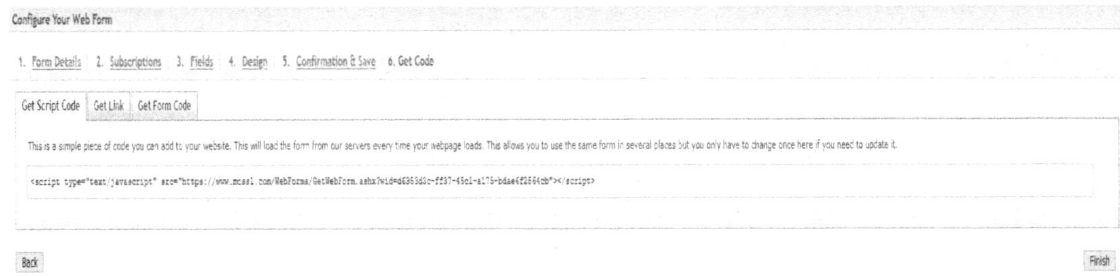

Opt-Ins

In order to get people onto your list you must first get them to "subscribe".

This is known as "opting-in" and there are strict rules governing the process.

Naturally, you want people on your lists but equally so, your prospects need to be protected. They need to be able to "opt-out" or un-subscribe from your list at any time.

You may come across the term "double opt-in" which means that once a person has opted-in they will be requested, by eMail, to confirm that they have requested information from you.

I prefer to go with the single opt-in method.

There are several ways that you can set up your opt-in process. But let's keep it simple.

The simplest place to position your opt-in box (as it's called) is on your squeeze pages. And there is a very good reason for my doing this. The reason being that when I create a web page, any web page, I want to achieve just one thing.

If that web page were a sales page, my "one thing" would be a 'call to action' for my visitors to buy.

In keeping with this philosophy, I want my squeeze pages to accomplish just one thing, and that is to get the visitor to opt in.

I don't want my visitors to get confused. Give your visitors more than one option on any of your web pages and you could confuse them.

And a confused mind will always say: "no".

As a minimum, you will require your prospect's first name and primary eMail address. Note: I didn't say: "name and eMail" there's a reason for that.

You want your prospect's first name (last name is optional) because your auto-responder has the ability to personalize every eMail that goes out with your prospect's first name. i.e. each eMail will be addressed: Dear John, and not Dear Friend, Dear Prospect, or Dear Mr. Smith.

Personalized eMails are just that … personal.

In return for your prospect giving you their contact details, you have to give them something in return.

In fact, if you don't offer something of value, it's unlikely that your prospect will give you his details. People these days are very discerning and selective. They are bombarded with eMail requests every day. You have to show that what you have to offer is different.

Any free giveaway you offer in return for an eMail is often referred to as an "ethical bribe" (a term which I hate but for now, I'll try to keep things simple).

A typical ethical bribe might be a free report or a series of sequentially delivered hints and tips – or both.

The bottom line being that they are now "on your list". They are now "subscribers".

Whatever it is that you offer, you should construct an auto-responder series that keeps your new subscribers interested. See below.

Unfortunately, it is not everyone that visits your squeeze page that will opt-in.

An opt-in rate of 40% or higher is considered to be good.

Yes, I find that strange as well. I would have thought that if the people visiting my website were "targeted" visitors (that's what I have supposedly paid for) then my opt-in rate should be more like 90%+

Very odd. I can only conclude that the visitors were not highly targeted.

But I also realize that people lead busy lives and just do not want to be bombarded with "yet another eMail" trying to pitch them.

Auto-Responders

Your newly subscribed prospect can receive, once you have set one up in your Total Business System account, an eMail at certain frequencies, decided by yourself. A good sequence would be for the first eMail message to go out immediately, the second message to go out after 1 day, the third after 3 days, and ultimately every week thereafter.

This sequential delivering of messages by eMail is known as an auto-responder series or sequence. The messages will be personalized with the prospect's first name. When the prospect receives your eMail it will give the impression that it is an eMail from you to him (which it is), but with a personal touch.

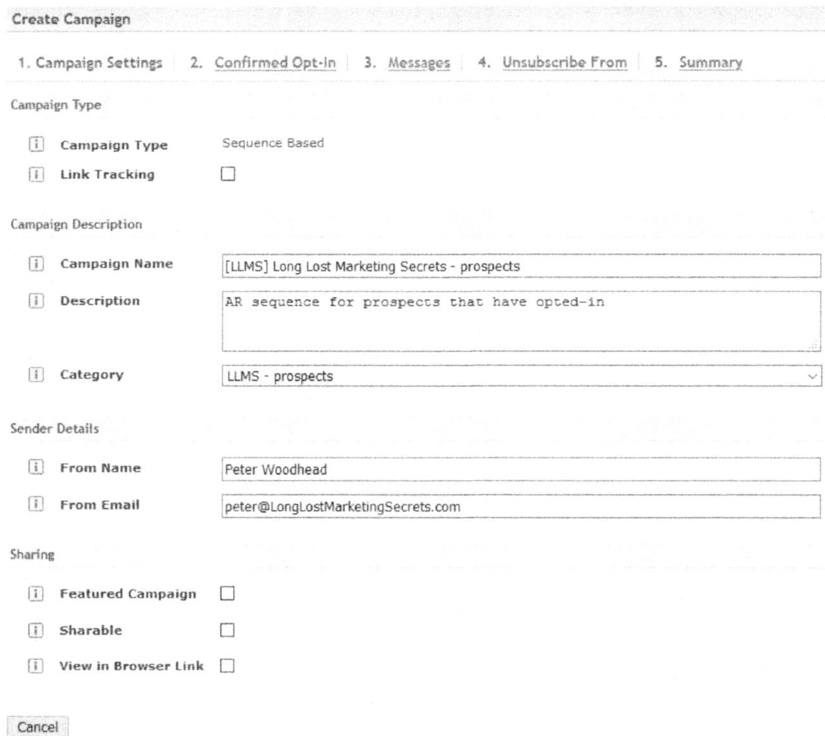

Similarly, if the visitor to your website were to buy your product, he too would have to give his name and primary eMail (otherwise how could you contact him?).

Your buyer though would go onto a different auto-responder because he is now a customer. The auto-responder that he would receive would show him how to consume the product he has just purchased.

You would end up with two lists: one for prospects and one for buyers.

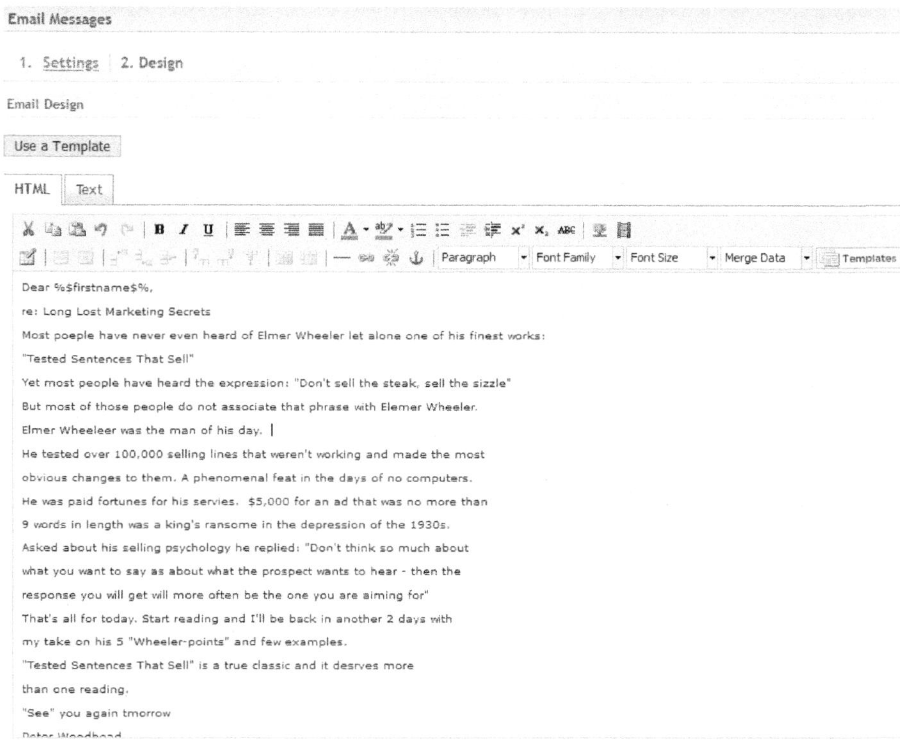

You should continue to correspond with both these groups (prospects and customers) – ad infinitum.

Keep adding to the auto-responder series that you have just created.

It is important to realize that it is not your lists that will ultimately determine your success. It is the "relationship" that you have with your lists.

Broadcasts

In addition to auto-responders, you can send one-off messages to the people on your lists.

These are known as "Broadcasts".

They are simple to set up.

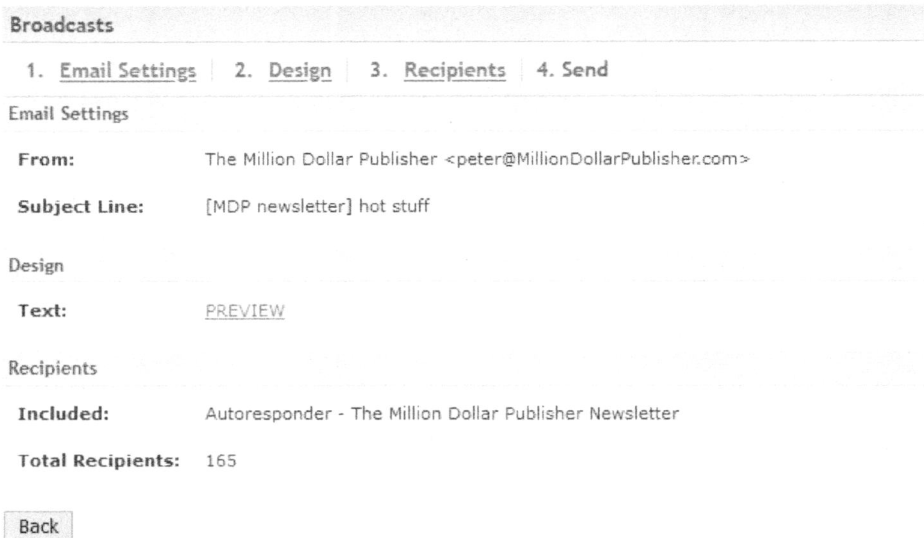

You would use Broadcasts if you wanted to contact people on your lists with a one-off message, for example, you were promoting a product for one of your marketing friends, or some newsworthy matter that you consider your lists should know about.

Tip: Keep your eMail messages short, on point, and useful. People are now very selective when it comes to subscribing to eMail lists.

You will have to work hard not only to get subscribers in the first place, but also to keep them.

Conclusion

Keeping in touch with your lists, is a never-ending pastime.

However, what I don't like are eMails that are too frequent, eMails that are far too long in content, and eMails that are always trying to sell me something.

I would think that most people share that view.

I don't care what the gurus say about length and frequency of eMails, I like to put myself in the shoes of my prospects and customers. If I were a subscriber to my lists, or any other lists, I do not like being constantly pitched to.

I get a lot of eMails each and every day.

I don't even open most of them.

I have one guy who not only eMails me almost daily, but a lot of the time two or three times a day. And, just to pee me off even more, he's always trying to sell something.

Rarely does he send an eMail that is full of useful content.

The "burn rate" on his list must be phenomenal.

Then I get an eMail from who I consider one of the "good" guys. He eMails me every day, but his eMails are short and bang on point. Something useful every time.

He tries to "pitch" me maybe once every two weeks. So guess what? I actually open and read every one of his eMails.

Most of the other eMails I receive are somewhere in between the two extremes I've mentioned above. The majority of them are boring.

Who should you imitate?

That depends. But I would rather gain the respect of my list than try to monetize it at every opportunity.

After the initial few weeks of sending my auto-responders out to my new contacts I generally send an auto response every week or every two weeks. Certainly no more frequently.

And if I want to send an urgent message, I will initiate a broadcast.

You must always bear in mind – it is the relationship that you have with your list that will determine your ultimate success.

It's not easy gathering new customers. It can be a very hard sell.

Doesn't it make sense to look after the ones you already have. It is far easier to sell again to an existing customer than it is to keep finding new ones.

Your Assignments for Step #14

You should know the drill by now.

Take action on every Step. For this Step you need to:

1. Sign up for an account with Total Business System. Go to:

   www.TotalBusiessSystem.com

2. Set up two auto-responders:
   - One for prospects
   - One for customers
3. Populate both auto-responders, initially for about 4 weeks and then continuously add to them. Never let them go to sleep.
4. Get, and read, the following books:
   - "Permission Marketing" by Seth Godin
   - "Overdeliver" by Brian Kurtz
   - "Oversubscribed" by Daniel Priestley

Step #15

Test That Your Website Converts Before Investing Heavily on Advertising

"It's much easier to double your business by doubling your conversion rate than by doubling your traffic"

Jeff Eisenberg

Introduction

Now you're really ready to roll!

Well, not quite.

Right now you've got a great offer. Irresistible even.

And your sales copy is as good as you could possibly make it (you think).

Your product is on the web for all to see, and ready to take orders.

But nobody knows it's there.

At this stage you just don't know how well it will do.

It's time to drive a gazillion visitors to your site. Right?

Wrong!

You may think that you've done a brilliant job at writing your sales copy, but have you?

Here's how to find out ...

You have to test the market.

Test The Market

You should drive 500-1000 highly targeted visitors to your website (and no more), usually using pay-per-click techniques (don't worry if you don't know how to do this right now – in Step #16 it will be explained in detail).

Measure how many sales you get.

Decide what's good and what's not so good.

If you were to get 100 visitors to your website and just one of them buys your offer, then you would have a 1% conversion rate. If two people bought your offer then your conversion rate would be 2% and so on.

- 1% is considered O.K.
- 2% is good
- 3% is very good
- 4% is terrific
- 5% is phenomenal. You would have hit the ball out of the park.

Now, what if it takes 200 visitors to get that one sale?

That would mean that your conversion rate would be 0,5%. Not a disaster, but it could be better.

You really need to drive a minimum of 500 visitors (but no more than 1000) to your website for this test but it is important that these visitors are not just any type of visitor. They need to be highly targeted visitors.

For example, if your niche is golf, there's no point sending people interested in fly fishing to your website. This would skew your results.

Assuming that you do drive targeted traffic to your webpage, what's the worst case scenario?

Obviously, if you make zero sales.

That should speak volumes to you.

What can you do? How can you fix it?

It's 99,99% certain that the problem would be your sales copy. It would just not be good enough.

It would need to be fixed.

Even if it meant a complete re-write.

I know it's easier said than done, but you really couldn't go any further until your sales letter converts.

Even if it converted at say, 1%, you must still keep tweaking your copy to make it better.

1,2% would be better than 1% and 1,3% would be better still.

Where to Find the Traffic

You can get your traffic from various sources. You will discover in the next Step almost 40 different ways to get traffic.

When I first got started in online information publishing, I was, quite rightly, told that there are only three ways to get traffic to your website. These are:

- You can Buy traffic
- You can Borrow traffic
- Or you can Build traffic

If you are very new to this business, maybe your only immediate option is to buy traffic. It might be difficult for you to borrow traffic as maybe you don't yet know anybody in your niche. And building traffic takes time.

With that in mind, your only real way to get some quick traffic is to invest a little capital.

Your options are limited as a "new kid on the block"

You could run a solo ad in an ezine or perform some other kind of advertising to get your 500-1000 visitors but a service called "pay-per-click" is just about the quickest and probably the easiest way to get those 500-1000 highly targeted visitors.

There are several places you can buy your traffic. I'll list just a few of them here. But my preference is to purchase ads from Google. When you have received your target of 500-1000 you just simply switch them off.

Here's just a handful of places you can buy ads from:

- Google
- Bing
- Facebook
- YouTube
- LinkedIn

The next Step (#16) goes into detail on how to set up Google Ads. It's not that complicated, but it has to be done in a certain way. I suppose you could say in a methodical way.

For the remainder of this Step I think it would be important to explain how to test and track the results you would receive from your advertising.

So really this Step needs to be read in conjunction with the next Step (#16).

Why You Must Test and Track

If you don't test and track, how can you make informed decisions about:

1. How much to spend on marketing or an ad campaign
2. If an ad campaign is giving you a positive or a negative investment return
3. If you can increase the average amount of money you receive from each visitor to your site

If you test and track you may be able to turn a losing marketing campaign into a profitable one. Or an average campaign into a winning one. Or maybe a winning campaign into a gold mine.

If you use the right tools then all the math is done for you, which leaves you free to analyze the results rather than wasting time. Or worse still, throwing good money after bad.

Before you even consider getting your feet wet testing and tracking, you need to be familiar with a few terms:

• Click Through Rate (CTR)	=	Clicks / Impressions x 100
• Sales Conversion Ratio	=	Sales / Clicks x 100
• Return on Investment (ROI)	=	(Sales – Cost) / Cost x 100
• Cost Per Conversion	=	Total Cost / Total Sales
• Average Visitor Value	=	Total Revenue / Number of Visitors
• Cost Per Conversion	=	Total Cost / Number of Visitors
• Average Profit Per Visitor	=	Average Visitor Value - Average Cost Per Visitor
• A / B Split Test	=	When you set up two pages, identical in every way except for just one difference. And then test one against the other.
• Statistical Relevancy	=	Expressed as a percentage of confidence level. A 95% confidence level means that, if you run the same test 100 times, it will turn out in favor of one result over another 95 times.
• Multi-Variant (or Taguchi testing)	=	An advance testing technique that allows you to test more than one variable at a time

The last two items in this list you will probably not need immediately, but they are included for completeness.

Some Common Mistakes

Here are some of the biggest mistakes that people make:

1. They don't test and track at all
2. They don't interpret the results that they get
3. They don't keep a record of what they've done
4. They listen to what "guru" marketers say and don't act on their own findings. Gurus that show results of what has worked for them does not mean that the same results will happen for you if you preform the same function. In fact, it's almost certain that your results will differ from theirs. Because each target market is different and each traffic source is different.
   I have learned over the years to do my own testing and tracking.

Hopefully by now you recognize the need to know what works and what doesn't work on your website. Let the people who really matter – your target market – answer the questions of your marketing.

Perhaps a few examples will make this a lot clearer:

Examples of Profitable Campaigns

A campaign is the advertising for just one of your keywords or keyword phrases. They are called campaigns because they are not just a simple advert placed on Google (or any other pay-per-click platform).

Campaigns (at least how I do them) comprise of ad groups of which each in turn consists of two ads. The two ads in each group are competing with each other (see later).

The whole process will be covered in detail in Step #16, but for now, just refer to the diagram below for a basic understanding.

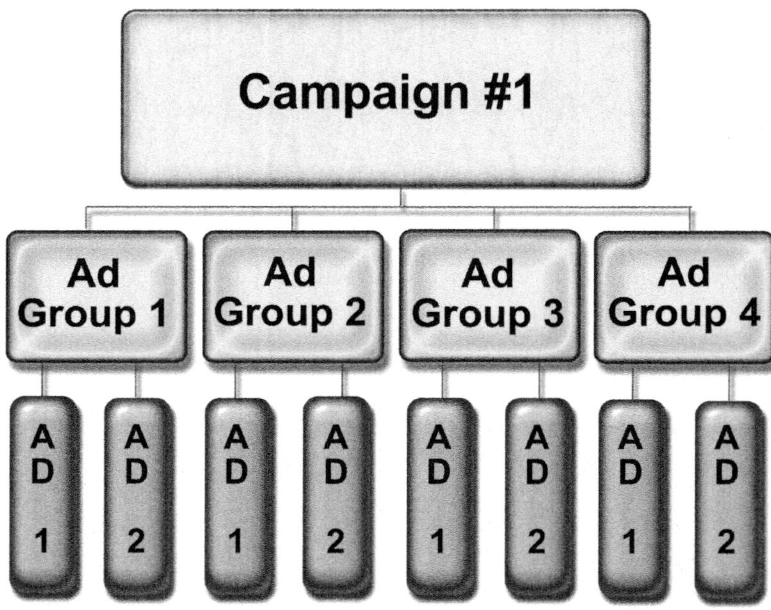

I like to give my ad campaigns a name. I find it much easier to identify my marketing especially if I have a lot of campaigns running.

Below are the results of one ad project that I ran. You will see that both the number of sales and the conversion rates differ. There is a reason for that. See below.

Rank	Campaign Name	Hits	Sales	Rate %
1	Marketing Secrets 2	68	20	29
2	Marketing Secrets 3	458	98	21
3	Marketing Secrets 8	439	38	9
4	Marketing and Advertising 2	26	1	4
5	Marketing and Advertising 4	291	10	3
6	Sales and Marketing 3	13210	112	1
7	Sales and Marketing 4	8649	85	1
8	Sales and Marketing 6	232	3	1
9	Marketing Secrets 10	6843	17	0,2

A real mixed bag.

The 'Marketing Secrets 2' campaign produced 20 sales from 68 clicks giving an excellent conversion rate of 29%

On delving deeper into this campaign the following statistics were revealed:

Sales Generated	20
Cost Per Sale	$0.32
Gross Profit Per Sale	$39.97
Net Profit Per Sale	$39.65

Yielding the following totals:

Current Cost of PPC	$0.09
Total Amount Invested	$6.48
Total Gross Profit	$799.4
Total Net Profit	$792.92
Conversion Ratio	29%
Return on Investment (ROI)	12236.4%

The above campaign showed a 'cost per sale' of 32 cents and a 'gross profit per sale' of $39.97 leaving a 'net profit' of $39.65. Which means that for investing $6.48 on traffic a 'total net profit' of $792.92 was made (on sales of $799.4) for a 'conversion ratio' of 29%. Which provided a fantastic 'Return on Investment' of 12236.4%

Now compare that campaign with the 'Sales and Marketing 4' campaign.

Here's what the stats looked like for that campaign:

Sales Generated	85
Cost Per Sale	$14.15
Gross Profit Per Sale	$39.97
Net Profit Per Sale	$25.82

Current Cost of PPC	$0.13
Total Amount Invested	$1202.76
Total Gross Profit	$3397.45
Total Net Profit	$2194.69
Conversion Ratio	0.9%
Return on Investment (ROI)	182.5%

Not as good as before but not bad …

More traffic was available for this campaign. There were 8649 visitors versus 68 for the first campaign. (In that first campaign there just wasn't enough traffic available).

In this 'Sales and Marketing 4' campaign, it produced a net profit of $2194.69 for an outlay of $1202.76

The point being, is that you need to understand that there are different traffic sources and different conversion metrics. Some, as in the first example, will have a really high conversion ratio and correspondingly low cost per conversion. It is usually on traffic sources where you can't generate significant traffic.

Whereas other campaigns, like the second example above, may generate lower conversion rates and a higher cost per conversion, but are still profitable.

Some campaigns however, will actually lose you money. And if you don't test – how would you know?

Example of a Losing Campaign

In this campaign, Marketing Secrets 10, 17 sales were made but it took 6843 clicks in order to get them.

Sales Generated	17
Cost Per Sale	$68.58
Gross Profit Per Sale	$39.97
Net Profit Per Sale	-$28.61

Current Cost of PPC	$0.17
Total Amount Invested	$1166.03
Total Gross Profit	$679.49
Total Net Profit	-$486.54
Conversion Ratio	0.2%
Return on Investment (ROI)	-41.7%

A classic example of why you must test.

How Does Testing Work?

Important parameters to measure are the number of successful actions. These could be number of clicks or number of purchases.

I am really interested in purchases more than number of clicks. I think purchases are a truer measure of success.

If you refer to the image earlier in this Step you will observe that all campaigns comprise of different ad groups and that all the ad groups contain two ads.

These two ads we can call ad 'A' and ad 'B' and the point is to monitor these two ads carefully.

The term used for this is called an A/B split test.

When you perform an A/B split test it is important to realize that you must only change one thing at a time.

Out of the two ads, one will perform better than the other. That better ad is called your "control" ad.

I will go deeper into changing ads in the next Step.

But the principle of A/B testing is applicable to your conversion testing.

Say you have driven your 500-1000 visitors to your website using Pay-Per-Click techniques, and you measured your conversion rate to be less than 1% - what action should you take?

Plenty.

There could be several reasons why you are not converting better. But I've been doing this long enough to know that it is 99.99% certain that it is your sales copy that is the problem.

It's not your fault. Probably nobody has ever explained it to you because they would not want you to hear the truth. (refer to Step #9). Copywriting is a very special skill and it can take many years to get good at doing it. But get good at it you must.

I know of dozens and dozens of wannabee marketers that have launched products and seen to their horror – zero sales.

I sympathize tremendously. They probably thought that they had done a half-decent job on their sales copy. How heart breaking must it have been to put in hours and hours of work getting online only to witness disastrous results.

I'm willing to wager that every one of those failures wanted so much to get their products online that they rushed the writing of their sales copy. I'd bet the ranch on it.

Those newbie marketers should take stock. It's not the end of the world. It can, and must, be corrected.

In the extreme event that no sales were made, it would look like a complete re-write of the sales copy. If a few sales were made – there's still hope.

The first thing to action is to find out exactly how many sales were made. Sales are the only true yardstick of success.

Using round figures, if 1000 highly targeted visitors were sent to your website, you should have expected to make between 10 and 20 sales (1% - 2%). Anything less than 10 requires immediate action.

Let's just re-cap all of that. If your 1000 highly targeted visitors produced no sales – it's a complete re-write of the sales copy. No questions.

If the 1000 highly targeted visitors resulted in between 10 and 20 sales, that's not bad. All that would now be required is to try and improve the sales copy still further.

If the 1000 highly targeted visitors resulted in less than 10 sales – the sales copy would require some serious modification if not a complete re-write.

Sidenote: If your sales fell into the "less than 10" category, I strongly suggest that you go no further in the marketing process. Correct the conversion problem now. No matter how long it would take you to improve your sales copy. Even if you have to study a copywriting home study course. Such an education would pay you back in spades and you would become part of the 3% copy-writing "royalty"

Now, assuming that your 1000 highly targeted visitors produced between 10 and 20 sales you are good to progress to the next step which is:

Improve Your Conversion Rate by Incremental Steps

Your website converts at say, 1%, are you happy with that?

You had better have answered "no" to that question. You should never be happy with your conversion rate. Always strive to improve it, even if your conversion rate is good. It will make such a difference to your bottom line.

You can improve your conversion rate by changing one thing at a time on your website. Before I list these, here are a few things on your website that you should be tracking and testing:

- The number of visitors to your website

- The average length of time visitors stay on your site
- The conversion rate of click throughs from your sales page to your order page
- The conversion rate of click throughs from your order page to Clickbank
- The ratio of completed purchases to those that only click through. (There is a phenomena known as "Shopping Cart Abandonment" and if this ratio is high you may have a serious problem)
- The percentage of people who opt-in to your prospect eMail list
- Average visitor value
- Cost of advertising (cost of ads, pay-per-click etc)
- Average profit per visitor

The above testing can be achieved by placing code on your website. The free program you would use to accomplish this is called Google Analytics. The installation of this is relatively simple to do (surprisingly) and it's free.

Now, back to improving your conversion rate.

Sales copy is the bane of most marketers. Most newbie marketers do not want to admit that sales copy is the key to success online. They seem to want to learn the hard way. Most never do "get it" and give up. That's a crying shame.

Bottom line is that you must get good at writing persuasive copy. Period.

We have all heard that your headline in your sales copy is probably the most important element. That's true, it is. But there are also other elements that can, and should be tested.

What is A/B Split Testing?

Below I have listed elements of a sales copy that can be A/B tested. The list is not limited but it is a decent start. If you perform an A/B test on all of these elements I would be very surprised if you do not incrementally increase your conversion rate after completing each one.

You may be wondering how you can get these A/B tests completed. There are many software programs that will perform this function for you and I like free when it gets the job done. One such program that is simple to implement is Google Optimize.

Make yourself ultra-familiar with this program. It will be responsible for making you a lot of money.

Here's the list of elements that you can, and should, A/B split test:

- Pre-Head
- Main Headline
- Sub-Headline
- Deck copy (if used)
- Opening Paragraph
- The Offer
- Short copy v. long copy
- Bonuses
- The Guarantee

- Call To Action
- The Price
- Adding Audio and/or Video to your website
- Adding Testimonials – the style, position, font
- Your Order Page
- Upsells
- Images – colors, borders, backgrounds, pictures, header
- Font types – in your headlines, calls to action, body type, size, color, drop capital for opening paragraph
- Order system – e.g. shopping cart v. Clickbank
- Order buttons, order links, order graphics
- The P.S.

Out of all these, the 3 most important are your Headline, your Price, and your P.S.

Conclusion

Testing works.

But what you need to understand is that it is the conversion rate of your Front End product that will ultimately determine your success in the online information publishing business.

Because it is your list of BUYERS that will determine your long-term achievement.

You need to build your customer list aggressively. Spend a lot of time trying to get your conversion rate as high as you possibly can. There is no ceiling. Don't stop, even if you find the process tedious.

You've seen what a difference your conversion rate can have on your bottom line. If you have a blockbuster Front End product it will look after you for many, many years to come.

If you have chosen a niche with a healthy following, there will be bags of potential customers for you to attract.

The larger your conversion rate the more customers you will acquire.

It really is a numbers game.

Remember – there's a new customer born every minute.

Your Assignments for Step #15

This could be the most important assignment of them all. Make sure that you spend some time on this ongoing activity.

1. Review your sales copy. Get someone experienced to take a critical look.
2. Drive a maximum of 1000 highly targeted visitors to your website for each test that you do.
3. Study all the metrics. What is your conversion rate?
    - Is it greater than 1%? Then congratulate yourself
    - Is it 1% or less? Then amend your sales copy and repeat the conversion rate test (i.e. drive 1000 more highly targeted visitors to your website)
    - Is it 0%? Then completely re-write your sales copy. Get some help if possible.
4. If your conversion rate was greater than 1%, implement A/B split testing on as many elements of your website as

possible, and re-test your conversion rate after each split test. Do this with at least 10 elements as listed.

5. Get, and read:

- "The Conversion Code" by Chris Smith
- "A/B Testing" by Dan Siroker

N.B. This is a lengthy assignment. But an important one. Do it right, get the right results and your success will be assured.

Step #16

Drive Massive Traffic To Your Website – Now That Your Website Converts Like Gang-busters

"The path to success is to take massive, determined action"

Tony Robbins

Introduction

Assuming that your conversion rate is 1% or greater (2% is preferred), it's now time to roll out your website to as many targeted visitors that you can get.

You can do this by various means.

You discovered in the previous Step that not all traffic sources are equal. You need the ones that give you the best bang for your buck.

As an insight into the different ways of driving traffic to your website, I will list them here in this introduction. If you want to major on one or more of the traffic generation techniques, and you should, then I suggest …

My preferred method of traffic generation. The one that I will expand upon in this Step. Which is: "Pay Per Click".

And even this method can be sub-divided into various individual providers.

I will concentrate on Google Ads (formerly known as Google Adwords) in this Step.

But first, here is a list of other traffic building techniques - should you want to explore further:

1. Advertise – Facebook Ads, Google Ads, Bing Ads, YouTube Ads, LinkedIn Ads,
2. Use Re-Targeting
3. Improve Your On-Page SEO (Search Engine Optimization)
4. Use Video on Your Web Pages
5. Launch a YouTube Channel
6. Host Webinars
7. Affiliate Marketing – Get an Army of Marketers working for you
8. Press Releases
9. Guest Blogging
10. Invite Others to Guest Blog on Your Site
11. Forum Posting
12. Get Active on Quora
13. Create Podcasts
14. Social Media
15. Post Content on LinkedIn

16. Share Images on Pinterest
17. Use Instagram
18. Add Social Share Buttons
19. Create a Facebook Page
20. Create a LinkedIn Page
21. Create Valuable Content People Will Link To
22. Link Internally
23. Make Your Website Responsive
24. Install and Use – Google Analytics
25. Optimize for Long-Tail Keywords
26. Always Research New Keywords
27. Spy on your Competition
28. Compose Powerful Headlines
29. Get To Know Influencers in Your Niche – and arrange JVs
30. Interview Influencers in Your Niche
31. Ensure Your Website Loads FAST
32. Write Knowledge Based Articles and Submit to Directories
33. Submit Content To Aggregator Sites
34. Add New Content Weekly
35. Keep Your Content Up-To-Date
36. Create Free Products and Tools
37. Outreach Marketing – Public Speaking, Give Interviews, Market to Haro,

Do I practice all of these?

It would be impractical for me, on my own, to get familiar with and use most of the above.

I have to admit that I am active in only about half a dozen of these traffic strategies.

I do, however, believe that, with the right organization, they could all be outsourced.

Think about that, use all the profits you make on the Front End to re-invest back into growing your lists.

If you are prepared to break-even on your front end in order to grow your lists, you will benefit when the time comes to marketing your back-end products by virtue of the fact that your customer lists will be much bigger than they might have been.

Look after your lists and they will look after you.

Burning your lists is, in my opinion, bad marketing. I know of plenty marketers that "burn" their lists. They arrogantly claim that more prospects sign up than those that unsubscribe. Making it a net gain for them, but I personally, do not like losing subscribers.

I think that burning your lists is a dreadful philosophy and suggest that you do not be any part of it.

Pay-Per-Click Advertising

This is my favorite way to market, at least in the beginning.

If you have just completed your first project, you will have nothing.

No lists. No partners. No rankings in the search engines.

Nobody knows you. Nobody knows of your new blockbuster website. Nobody will visit your website.

Organic traffic techniques (the 'Build It' traffic) will takes weeks, months, and even years to mature.

You also don't know anyone in your niche just yet, so being able to "borrow" traffic from partners is not yet an option for you.

You want traffic NOW. And as much as your niche can throw at you.

Cast your mind back to the early Steps of this resource and I re-iterated that what you are building here is an online information publishing business.

Not a hobby.

Up until now, the costs of setting up this business have been miniscule in comparison to a bricks and mortar business.

That is now about to change, that is if you want your business to take off.

I also touched on the subject of "scaling".

In the previous Step I outlined how to test if your website converts and not to settle for anything less than a 1% conversion rate. My preference is for 2% or more.

If you have done a sterling job on your sales copy, a 2% conversion rate is achievable and it is your cue to "break the bank" and throw as much traffic at your website as you can.

But not your own money. At least, not directly your own money.

The money that you “make” on your front end should all be ploughed back into buying traffic to pour into the top of your funnel (see Step #18).

Building your customer list, and building it as fast as you can should now be your priority.

Another priority needs to be the creation of your first Back End product (see Step #18). It's your Back End products (note the plural) where your big profits will be made.

I am now going to demonstrate to you, in detail, how you can drive all the traffic your website can handle. And, this is just ONE way of driving massive traffic to your website.

Look at the list of traffic methods given earlier – almost 40 of them.

Wow! You are going to have one heck of a problem. Your lists will grow exponentially. That's why I recommended to you a professional List Building software such as Total Business System. It can handle hundreds of thousands of names and eMails.

This is your business. You do not want to be associating yourself with some Micky Mouse free pieces of software. Do it right first time.

Right, now get ready for Mr.Toad's Wild Traffic Ride.

What is Pay-Per-Click?

Google Adwords (now called Google Ads) was one of the pioneers in this field.

We are all familiar with searching on Google. It's almost everybody's favorite search engine. What you see when you search are what are termed “organic” searches.

That is, when someone searches for a word or phrase, commonly referred to as a keyword or keyword phrase, Google returns pages and pages of results according to its algorithms.

Keywords and keyword phrases are listed in order of relevance – top to bottom. To be on the first page of Google would take months of painstaking SEO (Search Engine Optimization) – for popular keyword phrases.

But you haven't got the time, and probably not the expertise, to get all of your keywords and keyword phrases, on the first page of Google.

You want immediate search engine rankings.

Your only alternative is to buy your way in.

This is done by purchasing an advert that gets you to the top of the first page of Google. It's a display ad that sits there waiting for someone to "click" on it to see what you have to offer.

Once that someone "clicks" on your little display advert you will be charged for that privilege. Hence the term: Pay-Per-Click.

The key is to make your ad attractive to your visitors.

You may be wondering how much does this all cost? And you would be right to be concerned.

In order to get your advert on the first page of Google, you must "bid" against other marketers for that right. The higher you bid the better the chance you have of being "number one".

But it's not just about cost. Google likes to reward relevancy. It also likes to reward a good ad.

I will attempt to give here an understandable explanation of how pay-per-click works.

How Pay-Per-Click Works

There are many pay-per-click (PPC) advertising facilities on the internet, but Google Ads is by far the largest. Throughout this section I will refer only to Google Ads but the principle is the same for all the systems.

PPC operates on a model whereby the buyer (you and I) bid on keyword phrases to be shown on the advertisers' networks. But, the buyer will only pay for that ad if a visitor actually "clicks" on it.

The advertiser chooses where the buyers' ads will be positioned relative to one another. The higher the ad placing is decided by a number of factors – not just the price paid.

The main factors of how an ad is positioned in the search results is mainly determined by, but not limited to:

- the price paid
- the quality of the ad
- the relevance of the keyword phrase

To be more precise, positioning is based on Ad Rank which is a combination of two parameters:

1. The CPC (the Cost Per Click) – the price the buyer is willing to "bid"
2. The Quality Score – an assessment of the buyers':
    - Click Through Rate (CTR)
    - Keyword Relevance

- The quality of the landing page (the page that your visitor will arrive at when they click on your ad

So, just about everything regarding your ad is important. That's why you cannot afford to be complacent about PPC advertising. Either take the time to learn how to construct good PPC ads, or pay through the nose.

And you know what I think about those marketers that do not have the patience to do it right. They become members of the 97% club.

You simply have to learn how to be good at PPC advertising. How else are you going to send traffic to your website in the shortest possible time and at the cheapest possible price?

How To Improve Your PPC Ads

You know that Google rewards you for several factors, but suppose what you are doing does not get your ad high enough in their search ranking?

What can you do?

You can decide right here and now to do things right. Pay-per-click, like most things internet wise, is something not to be rushed.

By not taking the time to learn things properly, and Google Ads is just one strategy that has to be done properly. Otherwise ...

Do you like paying a lot of "stupidity tax"?

This is YOUR money we're talking about.

Here are a few pointers to help you improve your ads:

- Use a good keyword tool to help you select the right keyword phrases. Google is telling you what to look for with their Keyword Planner (and it's Free!)
- Google's "Quality Score" is how they rate the quality of your keyword phrases, landing pages, and campaigns
- Create landing pages that are optimized for relevant content with a clear call-to-action

Expanding a little on each of the above will give you a better idea of what Google is looking for.

BTW: Google employ professors and PhD qualified personnel. They work full-time at designing these systems and continually improving them. Doesn't common sense tell you that you have to play by their rules and never, ever, try to buck the system?

Keyword Research. You may have made a list of what you think are relevant keyword phrases. If so, well done!

However, compiling a list once is just the start. You need to be continually adding and deleting to that list. You need at all times to be using keyword phrases that will keep on giving you higher Click-Through-Rates. The phrases that you use need to be relevant.

Long-tail keywords can sometimes be the best. It is unlikely that other marketers will be using the exact same keywords as you.

Make no mistake about it, keyword research is a very important part of your strategy. Whatever niche you are in, you will have strong competition. Strive to be better than the rest.

Solution: spend time researching unique keyword phrases

Quality Score. Your Campaigns. Google reward you, in the form of cheaper costs per click, for creating good quality ads.

Campaigns need to be structured along the lines of that shown below.

Furthermore, you cannot simply create campaigns and leave them alone. They need continuous tweaking.

The diagram below shows how I set up my campaigns. You should do the same.

I give each campaign a unique name and feeding off that campaign name I set up about four ad groups.

Each of the ad groups comprising of two ads.

It is here, in those two ads, where the magic happens.

Each seen ad (see examples on the next page) comprises of:

- A headline - 25 characters max
- Two lines of text - 35 characters each max
- Display URL - 35 characters max

It is the wording of these two ads that will have a large contribution to your quality score.

This is how I structure all of my PPC campaigns, whether Google or other.

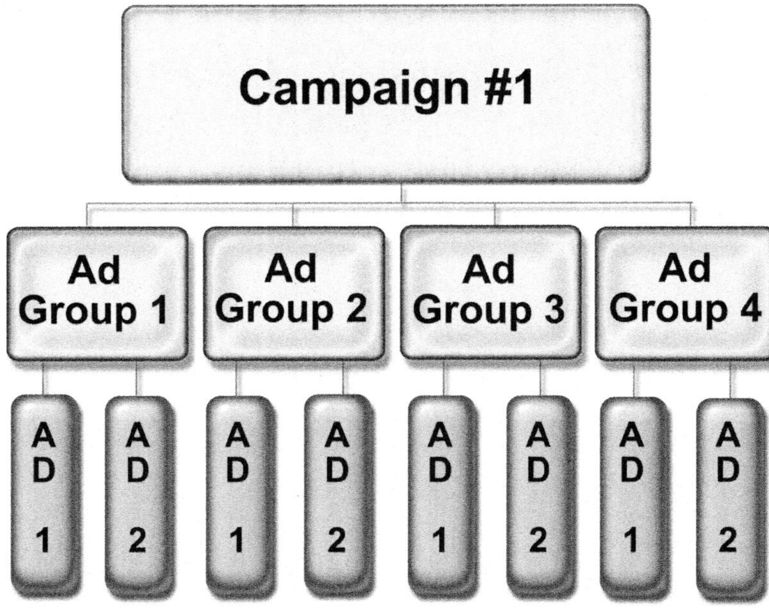

Two typical ads are shown below from an ad group within a campaign.

What you can't see on each ad is the destination URL, this has a generous character allowance of 1024 characters and is obviously where the visitor is directed upon clicking on your ad.

The two ads above are in competition with each other. Can you see the subtle difference between the two?

The visitors must have done because the second ad out-pulled the first by more than 3 to 1.

The second ad was easier on the eye, being lower case text against the first ad which was upper and lower case text.

Your next step would be to try and compose a new first ad to better that second ad. And so on and so forth.

Solution: get good at writing ads

Landing Pages. The 'destination URL' is where your potential customer arrives at once he has clicked on your ad. The relevance of this web page in relation to your keyword phrase will be scrutinized by the search engine.

The more relevant that your landing page is, the more the search engine will credit you, which will contribute to your overall ad rating.

Solution: get good at writing landing pages (a.k.a. squeeze pages) paying particular notice to the keyword content.

Conclusion

IF - your sales page converts at more than 1% (2% is preferable) then it's time for you to drive massive highly targeted traffic in the direction of your website.

I keep stressing the need to drive "highly targeted" traffic to your website. If you do not understand that term then go back a few Steps of this book and re-read them.

This is the Step where you are asked to invest serious money.

At the stage you are at with your fledgling information publishing business you have no list of your own, chances are that you don't know any big players in your niche, and your website is new and therefore not yet recognized by the various search engines.

You have no alternative but to buy your way to success – at least for now.

And the fastest, most cost-effective way to do that is to use Pay-Per-Click advertising – well it's my favorite.

Warning! Do not use PPC advertising half-heartedly. It will seriously bite you in the butt if you do.

And, you will pay a LOT of "stupidity tax"

If you can't get your head around the workings of PPC then pay someone to do it all for you. There are plenty of authorized PPC outsourcers out there.

Better still – get an outsourcer to teach you how to do it.

IF – your sales page converts at more than 1% then the best strategy, by a country mile, is to pour all of your Front End sales money back into MORE PPC advertising.

Depending on your niche – it should be quite some time before you exhaust your supply of "highly targeted" visitors.

And remember what P.T. Barnum is reputed to have said: "There is a new customer born every minute." If that is so, theoretically you will never run out of prospects.

Your Assignments for Step #16

It's getting technical now.

Here are your assignments for this Step:

1. If you haven't already done so, create a Google account NOW.
2. Get ultra-familiar with Google Ads. Then do the same for other PPC advertising platforms.
3. Set up ad campaigns as described in this Step. Get help if you need it.
4. Re-invest ALL your Front End sales profits (and more) into buying MORE highly targeted traffic. Do this all day and every day.
5. Outsource this work if you haven't got the time or inclination to do it yourself
6. Get, and read:
    - "Traffic Secrets" by Russel Brunson

Step #17

Continually Test, Tweak and Track – Always Try To Improve Your Conversion Rate

*"The only purpose of advertising is to make sales.
It is profitable or unprofitable according to its actual sales"*

Claude C. Hopkins

Introduction

You may have achieved that magical 1% (or better) conversion rate.

If so – many congratulations!

But you now need to continually try and improve this by making incremental changes. But, only by changing one thing at a time.

It may be the headline in your copy, it may be the price, or it may just be your P.S. But whatever it is, continually strive to get that 1% to 1,2%. Then on to 1,4% and so on.

Your target is 2% plus.

Never be satisfied with what you've got.

In this penultimate Step of the book, I would like to present you with 3 case studies, with a view to convincing you about testing and tracking.

The first case study is a straight forward campaign of placing a solo ad in an eZine.

The second being a Google Ad campaign

And the third a simple testing of two headlines.

I will finalise this Step by demonstrating that nearly all of your testing can be done for little or even no cost. There are a lot of tools that are free, as stated before.

And even paid for systems are not expensive. Especially when you consider how much money they can save you.

So, without further ado, let's take a look at the case studies.

Case Study #1

This was a product that was promoted by a solo ad placed in an eZine and distributed to 23,000 subscribers.

The cost of the ad was $74.95 and it returned $174.10 in just 3 days.

Not bad – spending $74.95 to get back $174.10. But what did the numbers tell me?

Let's take a look at what happened:

Number of eMails sent out	23,000
Number that clicked through to sales page	99
Number of sales	5
Sales conversion ratio	5.05%
Total Revenue from promotion	$174.10
Average visitor value	$1.76
Cost of solo eZine ad	$74.95

Cost of fulfilment (production and distribution)	$0.00
Gross profit	$99.15
Return on Investment (ROI)	132%
Average profit per visitor	$1.00

On analyzing the numbers the Average Visitor Value (Total Revenue/Total Number of Visitors) was $1.76

Meaning that, on average, $1.76 in revenue was made for every visitor drawn to the website.

Which equated to $1 profit for every visitor to the website.

Another way to look at this is by calculating the Return On Investment or ROI

$74.95 was turned into $174.10 in just 3 days. That's a Gross Profit of $99.15 giving a ROI of 132% in 3 days which is incredibly good.

At first glance, there were only 5 sales from 23,000 eMails, yet the conversion rate was a respectable 5.05% (99 clicks, 5 sales)

The ROI was more than acceptable at 132%.

Without any analysis, 5 sales from 23,000 eMails would have appeared awful.

Case Study #2

This Case Study was a Google Ad campaign.

There were 3 keyword phrases. All the stats are listed below:

Name of Ad	Clicks	Impr.	CTR %	Avg. CPC	Cost $	Conv. Rate %	Cost/ Conv	Sales
Train older dog	147	969	15.1	$0.09	13.29	1.36	$6.65	2
Train great dane	1,404	82,374	1.7	$0.08	116.65	1.28	$6.48	18
Obedience training	711	15,054	4.7	$0.17	123.24	1.13	$15.41	8

Taking the first keyword phrase (train older dog) with an average Cost Per Click of 9 cents, there were 969 impressions, with 147 clicks, resulting in a 15.1% Click Through Rate.

The low average Cost Per Click was due to the Click Through Rate being as high as it was. (Google reward you for a high CTR). The total cost being $13.29.

The Cost Per Conversion was $6.65.

That particular product sold for $39.97 with a Net Profit of $35.97.

With the 2 sales that were made the total revenue from that one keyword phrase was $71.94

The Total Revenue ($71.94) less the advertising cost ($13.29) revealed a Net Profit of $58.65.

Nothing special, but a profit nevertheless.

The second keyword phrase was 'train great dane'

The Average Cost Per Click was $0.08

There were 82,374 impressions with 1,404 clicks giving a Click Through Rate of 1.7% and 18 sales were made.

This produced a Total Cost of $116.65 with a conversion rate of 1.28% and a Cost Per Conversion of $6.48

The product sold for $19.97 giving a Total Gross Profit of $359.46 and a Net Profit of $242.81 ($359.46 - $116.65)

And lastly, the third keyword phrase was 'obedience training'

The average Cost Per Click was $0.17. The phrase had 15,054 impressions with 711 clicks producing a Click Through Rate of 4.7%

The Total Cost of advertising worked out at $123.24

This product sold at $35.97 producing a Gross Profit of $287.76 and a Net Profit of $164.52 with a respectable Conversion Rate of 1.13% and a Cost Per Conversion of $15.41

This latter keyword phrase converted with a Click Through Rate of 4.7%.

That's pretty good. And Google rewards you for "pretty good" CTRs in the form of higher placings.

With that fact in mind, can you do even better still?

Take the keyword phrase "obedience training"

In this case study it received a grand total number of clicks of 711

But keyword phrases can be bid on 3 different variations. These are (for this particular keyword phrase):

- "obedience training"
- [obedience training]
- obedience training

Google does this so that you can optimize your placing of keyword phrases.

The meaning of each of these phrases is as follows:

- "obedience training" means a match on the phrase
- [obedience training] means an exact match
- obedience training means it's a broad match

Now see how those 711 clicks were apportioned:

Keyword	Click	Impr.	CTR %	Avg. CPC	Cost $	Conv Rate %	Cost/ conv	Sales
"obedience training"	189	5,897	3.2	$0.17	32.04	1.59	$10.68	3
[obedience training]	360	3,666	9.8	$0.17	58.16	0.83	$19.39	3
obedience training	63	1,851	3.4	$0.18	10.72	0.00	$0	0

One other keyword phrase completed this campaign: [dog obedience training] with the following results:

[dog obedience training]	99	3,640	2.7	$0.23	22.32	2.02	$11.16	2

What can we conclude from the above?

The fourth keyword phrase converted at 2.02% whereas the broad match keyword (obedience training) didn't convert at all.

Three of the four keyword phrases showed a profit and the campaign would have done even better had the broad match keyword phrase been deleted. That broad match had 63 clicks, at an average cost of 18 cents, with zero results.

The idea being now to concentrate on the three ads that did show a profit. Trying all the time to "beat the control"

Here are two examples:

Obedience Training Secret
Learn How To Get Your Dog To Obey
Your Every Command. Start today.
www.DogTrainingZone.com

105 Clicks | 2.7% CTR | $0.22 CPC
Served - 3.4%

Obedience Training Secret
Learn how to get your dog to obey
your every command. Start today.
www.DogTrainingZone.com

360 Clicks | 3.5% CTR | $0.21 CPC
Served - 9.1% [more info]

You will notice that the second ad gets more clicks than the first and it also has a better CTR. Just what Google likes.

Our job as marketers, is to keep trying to improve that CTR

Without adding the code to your website you would never know any of the aforementioned information. It's invaluable and it's free.

Merely placing the ads and taking the money would be lazy marketing. Delve deeper and find ads that don't perform – delete these and try to improve the others. Then watch your profits zoom.

Case Study #3

This case study is something you should do on a regular basis. In fact, all of the time. It is:

A/B split testing

It's always best to use examples. The following example is of two headlines:

Headline 'A'

"How to Have Your Dog or Puppy Obey Your Every Command With The Easiest, Step-By-Step Dog Training System Available – Start Seeing Results The Very First Day!"

Headline 'B'

"How To Easily Transform Your Stubborn, Out-Of-Control Dog Into A Loyal And Affectionate 'Best Friend' That Obeys Your Every Command – And Start Seeing Results The Very First Day!"

Now ... test yourself. Which of the above two headlines do you think was the best?

The result may surprise you. Which is why you MUST put the question to the people that matter – your target market.

First, take a look at the statistics for the overall campaign:

Sales generated	20
Cost per Sale	$0.32
Gross Profit per Sales	$39.97
Net Profit per Sale	$39.65

And the totals:

Current Cost (PPC)	$0.09
Total amount invested	$6.48
Total Gross Profit	$799.40
Total Net Profit	$792.92
Conversion Rate	27.8%
ROI	12236.4%

You saw these figures in a previous Step but now let's observe the detailed results from each headline.

Headline 'A' attracted 36 clicks ($3.24/$0.09) but didn't make a single sale.

Sales generated	0
Cost per Sale	$0.00
Gross Profit per Sale	$0.00
Net Profit per sale	$0.00

Current Cost (PPC)	$0.09
Total amount invested	$3.24
Total Gross Profit	$0
Total Net Profit	-$3.24
Conversion Rate	0%
ROI	-100%

Showing a loss of $3.24

Headline 'B' had 34 clicks – but look at the stats for this headline:

Sales Generated	20
Cost Per Sales	$0.15
Gross Profit per Sale	$39.97
Net Profit per Sale	$39.72

And the totals:

Current Cost (PPC)	$0.09
Total amount invested	$3.06
Total Gross Profit	$799.40
Total Net Profit	$796.34
Conversion Rate	62.5%
ROI	26024.2%

This shows a total of 20 sales from just 34 clicks. $3.06 was invested to bring in $799.40 with a profit of $796.34. A conversion rate of 62.5%

The ROI was a staggering 26024.2%. Beats Real Estate and Wall Street.

What was it that made the difference?

Just one simple tweak to the headline – but you wouldn't know until you tested. That's the whole point. You gotta test.

Those 20 sales resulted in almost $800 in profits, as opposed to zero sales and a loss from the other headline.

How could you have known this, had you not tested it? There's no way you could have.

Conclusion

It is a very clear message.

You gotta test.

Get ultra-familiar with testing. It will be your best friend.

And the best thing is – for the most part – it's FREE!

This Step has highlighted 3 ways that you can advertize your products. There are many more.

Information Publishing is an art and a science. And you must learn it if you want to achieve massive success. Why be a Mr. or Mrs. Average? Take the time and effort to be good at testing and it will serve you well.

I rank it second as important to copywriting in this business. It is a large chunk of that giant jigsaw puzzle.

Make sure that you don't lose a few of the pieces.

Your Assignments for Step #17

1. If you haven't done so already, get yourself an account at Google.
2. Get yourself acquainted with Google Analytics and Google Optimize
3. Start your testing experiences by experimenting with 3 types of advertising.
4. Hint: this Step showed you 3 case studies.
5. Split-Testing will be a part of your marketing arsenal from now on. Investigate various split testing tools by going to the link:

https://westwooddigitalmarketing.com/blog/top-10-split-testing-tools

6. Get, and read:
    - "Making Websites Win" by Dr. Karl Blanks and Ben Jesson

Step #18

Create Bigger and More Expensive Back End Products For Your Ever-Growing List of Buyers

"In sales: a funnel works best when it's full and consistently being filled; hence, the more a funnel is funnelling, the more fun it is to funnel"

Paulette Smith

Introduction

I know – it's sad. This is the last Step of the book.

You have come a long way in the last 17 Steps.

But I want to be honest with you. Up until now, you have only scratched the surface.

Creating your Front End product will not make you a millionaire. If indeed, that's what you aspire to. But it is a darn good start.

You may have heard about people prattling on about "Funnels" – what are they?

Put very crudely, your Funnel will be the path that your visitor takes on first becoming one of your prospects. He then becomes a customer, and then a repeat customer buying ever increasing valued products from you.

The journey of your prospect can best be summed up by the diagram in the next section.

The Sales Funnel

A very simplified way to discover how you can build your online information publishing empire is by understanding the Sales Funnel.

Take note of the diagram on the next page.

The funnel system of marketing depicts you offering to your prospects, who then become customers, larger and more expensive products and services.

The concept being that you bring in prospects and new customers into your business and then give them more and more ways to spend more money with you.

It all starts with the top of the funnel where you first get them on board.

In the case of prospects, you have convinced them to give you their first name and primary eMail address in exchange for an "ethical bribe".

In the case of a new customer, they will have entered your funnel by buying your front-end product at say, $37 or maybe they came in by the "back door" and invested under $10 for your "self-liquidating offer".

Your next tasks are to convert your prospects into first time buyers and to get your new customers to buy a higher-priced product.

----Your Prospects Enter Here ----

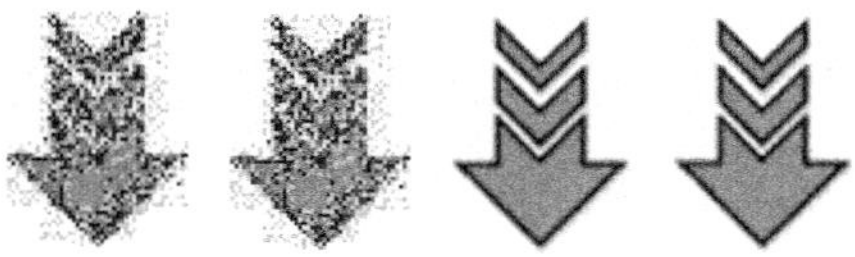

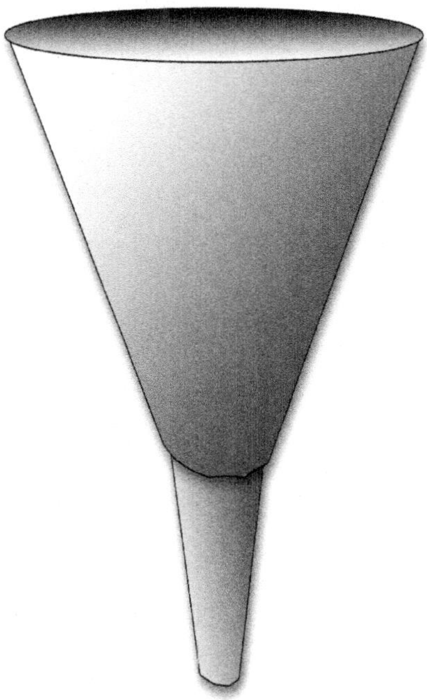

Free Reports/eCourse ("ethical bribe")	Free
"Self-liquidating offer"	under $10
Books	$17-$27
eBooks	$47
Manuals	$97+
CDs/CD ROMs	$97
DVDs	$247-$997
Webinars	$297
Membership Sites	$17-$97/m
Home Study Courses	$497
Workshops/Seminars	$$697-$5K
Coaching	$$$
Consulting	$$$
Whole Enchilada	$10K+

Once you have secured new customers on board, it is your job, through the relationship that you establish with your customers, to sell them the next product in your line.

Your new product may be a piece of software priced at $197.

Then you might create a membership site at $97 per month.

After that, an online or offline home study course at $497

Then a workshop/seminar or consulting at $1997

Perhaps you have enough experience to sell one-to-one mentoring at $4997

If you can coax onboard loyal customers that buy everything from you, the sky's the limit. They could spend $20,000 or more with you.

It All Starts By Bringing In People at Little or No Cost

This business model concentrates on bringing in a lot of prospects and new customers at a very low cost. In the case of prospects – at no cost.

Either way, those people end up on your lists.

Then, as you focus on marketing more sophisticated products to your lists, you quite naturally sell less products but to a group of people who have the ability to pay the higher prices.

You automatically focus on serving the needs of this more discerning customer and create products that they want to buy.

It may be that thousands of people enter your funnel at the top and just don't want to buy any higher priced products. But that's alright. It's a numbers game.

Some will want to buy more. Most won't.

As you grow, a handful of people will become "advocates" for you and the information that you provide.

Using the systems that I have outlined previously, you should have little problem in churning out the quantity of product that your insatiable customers want.

People Will Buy What They Want

If you have researched your niche properly, there will always be people willing to buy your information. It is so much easier to develop and sell information to those that already want to buy it.

You may not find it believable but, it has been proven that people will spend money to reach a goal more often than they will spend money to solve a problem.

And if you are stuck for knowing what your customers want. Ask them.

Or run a small ad offering a product you are thinking of producing. If the response is poor, you'll know it won't do well. And you will know it before you spend time, money and effort creating that product.

Avoid spending resources on products you think people will want.

The Lifetime Value of Your Customer

In short, you need to know how much you can afford to spend in bringing a new customer into your funnel. You do this by calculating the Lifetime Value of Your Customer.

The Lifetime Value of Your Customer is the total amount that a customer spends with you over the time that they remain one of your customers.

If you have 1000 customers in your funnel and 3 of them spend $20,000 and the remaining 997 customers spend a total of $10,000. How much would you pay to get 1000 new customers, knowing that you will make on average, $30K from them?

It really is a numbers game.

Your "Back End" products

Your "Back-End" products may be all manner of things ranging from a physical product to four-figure seminars and workshops.

Different people learn through different modalities.

This alone gives you ideas:

- Some people like to read
- Some like to listen (e.g. audio)
- Some like to watch (e.g. video)
- Others like to see and do (workshops)
- Many like to experience (live events)
- A few like to work one-on-one (coaching)

Consider this: What is your perceived value of a book? $6, $10, $16, maybe $20/$30 tops. But instead of selling the book for $20, present the same information in a different format.

Now call it a manual. Make it spiral bound, or in a smart ring binder.

Now what is the perceived value?

Believe it or believe it not, you would be able to sell that manual for $97.

Change that “manual” into a Home Study Course and you could market that product for $497 if it was well-presented.

Maybe in a future revision to this book, I could prove that theory to you. Would you then believe it?

Here’s a list of possibilities that you could create for your Back-End products, together with their price points:

- Manuals - $97+
- CDs/CD ROMs - $97
- DVDs - $247-$997 (about $50 per DVD)
- Teleseminars/Webinars - $297+
- Membership sites - $17-$97 per month
- Home Study Courses - $497
- Workshops/Seminars - $697-$4,997
- Coaching - $$$
- Consulting - $$$
- The Whole Enchilada - $10,000+

When you start out as an online information publisher, people don’t know you. So they are unlikely to buy a $997 product from you, are they?

You have to start with a low-priced product, sometimes even a free product (such as a report), and gain their confidence and trust. Then, when they get to know you, like you, and trust you, they will buy your higher priced products.

You are trying to build a customer base for life. This is not a Get Rich Quick type of business. Far from it. This is a ‘do it right at the beginning and get rich later’ type of business.

What the Funnel System does is get you to think of price points, not products.

In today's hi-tech world, having simple products like reports in downloadable format, makes sense. PDF (Portable Document File) is the recognized format for such products and PDFs can be read by any computer platform and any operating system.

Whether you have a PC, a Mac, or any other operating system, a PDF document can be read. Convenient, eh?

And, PDFs are virus-free.

Other Peoples' Products (OPP)

Before I wrap up this Step, I feel obligated to mention Other Peoples' Products.

Earlier in the book I stated that I have basically four ways that I "create" my products. Actually, I could add a fifth method but it is one that I wouldn't use personally.

To re-cap, here are the four methods I have used:

1. Public Domain material
2. Private Label Rights
3. Licensed products
4. Outsourcing

And the fifth way I could obtain material and sell it on would be by acting as an affiliate for someone's product. I mention this in passing so that you know what is possible, I personally hardly ever use it. Why?

Because I like all my products to have a certain uniqueness about them. By acting as an affiliate, I would be obliged to sell someone's product without being able to change it. Even slightly.

I would be competing with dozens of other marketers. No thanks. It's not for me.

And for the same reason, I suggest it is not for you.

You need products that stand out from the crowd. Not "me too" products.

I have covered Public Domain content in some detail. Briefly mentioned Private Label Rights. And stated that I use Outsourcing to get the jobs done that I can't do, or jobs that I don't want to do.

That leaves Licensing products.

Licensing products I generally use for my Back End products.

I have licensed books, software, CDs, DVDs, and Home Study Courses. And the best part is, it is not that expensive. I have picked up licenses for really good products for under $500. All you need is a little bit of imagination.

Yes, you will be competing with other marketers but this time at the higher end of the price spectrum.

Where I look to be different is that I like to provide value. I have done this by using Licensed products as part of a bundle of products.

Usually, all the Licensed Products I have acquired have been physical products.

For example, say I have licensed a set of DVDs in the golf niche. What I have done to make my package unique is bundle those DVDs with books from the Public Domain. But not just books for the sake of books.

I happen to have found some real gems in the Public Domain. Works by famous golfers. Works that they forgot to renew, which is good for the likes of us. We can just legally take these works, modify them (which I prefer to do) and profit from them.

I can read your mind as you are reading this. You're thinking: "It all sounds great, but where can I find these Licensed Products?"

Depending on the niche you are in, will depend on what is available. Some niches are open to licensed products some less so.

The first place I search for are the big players in my niche. Look at their marketing materials. Some openly offer the licensing of their products.

Even if they don't openly advertise their products for licensing, don't give up at that. Contact them. If you don't ask, you don't get.

I remember a few years back I was searching for a Public Domain work in the financial niche. I found this book by a very well-known investment guru published in 1923. It was a classic work and still sought after today.

At the time, I thought it could possibly be in the Public Domain, but no, the work had been renewed. But I really wanted the book for part of an investment bundle I was putting together – so I contacted the publishers directly.

I was both surprised and pleased that they agreed to license the product to me for a fraction of retail price. If you don't ask you don't get. I still sell that work to this day.

Finally, dig a little deeper. Use our best friend – Google.

Search for "Licensed Products in ***your niche***"

I have found that when I search for licensed products - the deeper I delve, the more successful I become. It's too easy to give up too soon. Persistence is the key.

Conclusion

Don't think it's at all possible?

Then think again.

My background was engineering. Not a bad profession but very demanding. I was always away from home.

Great if you like travelling. Not so great if you just want to be with your family.

Sure, I'd seen parts of the world that other people only read about.

I wanted out.

I knew that there were lots of people making a killing with this internet marketing thing. And I longed to be one of them.

Long story short … within 2 short years of launching my first product I had produced products in four different niches.

And around that same time I had organized, well into double figures, seminars with various online marketers. Most notably – Yanik Silver, Jim Edwards and the late, great, Ted Nicholas.

I also hosted plenty of my own workshops.

My range of Back-End products covered live events, digital and physical products.

The acquaintances that I met along the way were like some who's who of marketing, many of whom I did joint ventures with.

I'm not telling you this to blow my own trumpet but to let you know that anything is possible. Anything.

Your Assignments for Step #18

Just because this happens to be the last Step of the book, it doesn't mean that you now have everything you require to become a fully-fledged information publisher.

You're still a neophyte.

It also means that you are not going to get away with no assignment. Get used to the idea that there is always something to do.

Here're your assignments for this final Step:

1. If you haven't already done so, decide what your Back End product(s) are likely to be. Even when you are creating your Front End offer, always have in mind your Back End.

   You will have chosen your niche with care and plenty of research (right?), providing you have offered great value with your Front End offer, you should have no problem with your Back End offers.

2. Go out of your way to find a Licensed Product. Do not give up until you have found something. You will be ready for publishing your Back End product sooner than you think, so start planning now!

3. Don't think product. Think bundle. Be unique. Aim to deliver 10x value.

Every Step of this book has suggested reading matter for you. Should you obtain every resource that I have listed? Well, maybe not all at once but it is extremely advisable that you build a good library of your own.

Over the past century or so, there have been some terrific marketers. Marketers of today take a lot of their ideas from these guys. Now you can do the same by getting your hands on their works. They are still available.

See my resource: Lost Secrets of Marketing Legends It's free and can be found with the rest of the free resources available in this book.

Conclusion: This is Just The Beginning

Congratulations!

If you have read every Step of this book.

Many, many congratulations if you have completed any, or all of the assignments.

In a book of 300 or so pages, it is impossible to say everything that is needed to be said. For example, I have only made a passing comment about Social Media.

I view Social Media as a rapidly-growing source of traffic. Marketers like ourselves should get familiar with it.

Social Media apart, I'd like to think that this book has been a good introduction to the world of online information publishing.

If you have consumed the whole book then you will by now probably agree with me that it isn't an easy subject if you want to do it right.

It takes time. It takes effort. And it takes a little resource – although, with the exception of paid advertising, I intentionally kept any costs down to a bare minimum.

I have slipped in this conclusion to the book to remind you, if you had not realized it already, that if you sincerely want to be a success at online information publishing then there is so much more that you need to know.

The contents of this book have given you the introduction. But this book alone is just the tip of the iceberg.

If you really want to get serious about this topic you need to add to your education.

Reading the recommended books is a great start, but that's an ongoing thing that you should be doing anyway. And just reading books on internet marketing can make you more than a little narrow-focused.

I read, on average, one book a week. But the topics of my reading are not just books that are internet related. My pet subject is history – I reckon I read more history books than I do marketing books. I also have interests in music, sport, travel, finance, autobiographies, and the list could go on.

Reading really can help you on your way to being a better copywriter, and you should know by now what I think about being good at copywriting:

Poor copywriting = limited success

IMHO you should consume a good course on the subject of writing good, persuasive copy. Details of which were included at the end of Step #9.

Now that you have completed the book, can you begin to see why 97% of those that try this internet marketing thingy – fail?

There never has been such a thing as a free lunch – and there never will be.

The secret (if it is a secret) to success is honest endeavor.

And as one former US President was famous for quoting: "Nothing in this world can take the place of persistence"

Never, ever quit!

My final message for you is that if you want to take your education in online information publishing to the next level, I strongly suggest that you take a look at my 52 week online course.

It is the nearest thing to guaranteeing your online marketing success that I've come across. But …

… access to Million Dollar Publisher is limited. I restrict access to a limited number of students at any one time. Check it out by going to the following link:

- https://www.MillionDollarPublisher.com

The resources mentioned in the book that are yours free to download can be accessed by going to:

https://www.TheMillionDollarPublisher.com/
Special_reports_101.html

P.S. And just as you thought that I'd gone away …

… I have one final tip for you: since the very beginning, I have practiced one thing every day. No matter how long the day has been. No matter what else I have had to do. No matter how I felt. No matter how tired I was. No matter where I was.

I always did, and still do, this one thing:

"Make sure that you do something pro-active every single day. It does not matter how big or how small that 'something' may be – just do it. It might be the writing of a few messages for an auto-responder series, or it might just be researching keywords. Whatever!

Do that one thing EVERY day. Without fail. At the end of 6 months, you will be surprised at how much difference that small contribution will have made to your overall progress."

Printed in Great Britain
by Amazon

80403419R00174